Jean Allan Owen

The story of Hawaii

Jean Allan Owen
The story of Hawaii
ISBN/EAN: 9783337821234
Printed in Europe, USA, Canada, Australia, Japan
Cover: Foto ©ninafisch / pixelio.de

More available books at **www.hansebooks.com**

THE
STORY OF HAWAII

BY

JEAN A. OWEN

(MRS. VISGER)

Author of "Forest, Field, and Fell," "The Country Month
by Month," &c., and Editor of the books
signed "A Son of the Marshes"

LONDON AND NEW YORK
HARPER & BROTHERS
45 ALBEMARLE STREET, W.
1898

PREFACE

IN one of his poems, Matthew Arnold writes of man as a wanderer "born on a ship, on the breast of the river of Time," and he adds, "only the tract where he sails he wots of; only the thoughts raised by the objects he passes, are his."

I have been in a literal sense a wanderer. Having spent some years in Oahu, the chief of the Hawaiian Islands, besides having been in close and regular correspondence with English residents, my sisters, ever since, I may claim to know something of Hawaii and its people; and also of those from other countries who have, many of them for three generations, made their homes there, and who now have large vested interests in the Islands.

Hawaii lies between 18° 54′ and 22° 15′ of north latitude, that is just within the tropics. I have been struck with the ignorance of otherwise intelligent persons in our own country as to what they often vaguely designate as the South Sea Islands. I am constantly asked questions which show that Tahiti, the Fijis, Samoa, and, what are by many still called the Sandwich Islands, are all vaguely mixed up in the minds of some who seem to imagine they are within a few days' sail of each other, instead of thousands of miles apart. From Tahiti they are 2380 miles distant, from the Fijian Islands 2700, from Samoa 2290. They are the only group of islands of any importance in the North Pacific Ocean, and they have been declared by a naval expert to be "the key to the entire Pacific."

Since Hawaii has become a bone of international contention, some account of these lovely islands, "the Paradise of the Pacific," may be acceptable to many. I have to acknowledge my indebtedness to Professor Alexander in his "History of Hawaii," to Mrs. Judd's interesting diary, published by her son, Mr. A. F. Judd, to Mr. Thrum's "Annual for 1897," to Mrs. Emma Nakuina, a Hawaiian lady living in Honolulu, and to Professor A. B. Lyons.

JEAN A. OWEN.

London, 1898.

CONTENTS

CHAP.		PAGE
I.	THE EIGHT INHABITED ISLANDS	1
II.	PLANT LIFE OF THE HAWAIIAN ISLANDS	30
III.	ORIGIN OF THE HAWAIIANS; THEIR EARLY CUSTOMS AND RITES	49
IV.	THE GODDESS OF THE GREAT VOLCANOES	89
V.	THE FIRST KINGS OF UNITED HAWAII	102
VI.	A PRACTICAL MISSION	129
VII.	KAMEHAMEHA III., HIS ADVISERS, AND HIS AGGRESSORS	146
VIII.	PRINCE ALEXANDER, PRINCE LOT, AND LUNALILO	184
IX.	THE LAST OF HAWAIIAN ROYALTY	191
X.	THE HAWAII OF TO-DAY	208

LIST OF ILLUSTRATIONS

	Page
A Bridge on an old Plantation . . *Frontispiece*	
A Native Grass Hut	6
Collection of Hawaiian Curiosities made by the Dowager Queen Kapiolani	82
A Feast in Native Style	86
A difficult Landing Stage	138
The Dowager Queen Emma	184
King Lunalilo, "Prince Bill"	190
Hana Harbour, Naui	210

The Story of Hawaii

CHAPTER I

THE EIGHT INHABITED ISLANDS

There are eight islands which are capable of being inhabited and cultivated. Of these Hawaii is the largest, although Honolulu, the capital, is on the island of Oahu. Hawaii has an area of 4210 square miles, and its mountains rise to an elevation of 13,805 feet above the sea.

Kona is a fine coffee-growing district on Hawaii, and a great health resort of the Honolulu folks. So much in request is the land which is suitable for coffee, that it is difficult now to buy or rent any in that district. This berry is grown on soil that is unsuited for sugar-canes or rice. Its cultivation is followed by small as well as large farmers, some planters having as many as 200,000 trees, others so small a concern as one acre planted. The oranges, too, grown in this district are very fine and rich in flavour.

The town of Hilo has grown rapidly of late years. It has a most beautiful bay. Tall tree-ferns line the roadways, and stately coco-palms, with yellow waving tresses, fringe the shore. Cascades leap down clefts in the steep rocky mountain sides, and from the deck of some little coaster the eye covers a wonderful landscape, beginning with the full blue of the water, looking over the fronded palms, and up the verdant fruitful slopes, until it rests on the snow-covered summits of Mauna Kea and Mauna Loa.

If any one would know what a ride on horseback along the shores and across the valleys and torrents out from Hilo is like, let him read Miss Bird's account of this. I rode later over the same district, and can endorse her enthusiastic description of all most fully.

Our first voyage thither in a small coasting schooner was very primitive. It ought to have taken two days from Honolulu to Hilo Bay, but we were five on the way: three days we spent in trying to round the point just before entering the bay. As usual, my husband had preferred sail to steam.

The captain of our schooner was a native, short and broad, with a bald head and strong face. He reminded me of the conventional idea of Saint Peter. Next to him, of course, in importance, was the mate; but this mate was an immensely tall and fat woman, his most loving wife. The steward was also cook, and there were three sailors. The cabin was tiny, just holding a table, round which ran a long cushioned bench; on this we sat at meals and slept at night. *We* included the captain and his wife, who lay on each side of the door, a boorish farmer from the foot hills of Mariposa, California, my husband and myself. The stout forms of the captain and his wife seemed to fill up the cabin, and they snored in a loud duet all through the night.

They had a pet in the shape of an ancient white rooster. This old cock was always tied to a nail by the cabin door, with a string that allowed it to wander and perch on the side of the vessel and, weather permitting, on the mainmast. After two days the weather began to be wet and squally. Nothing kept my husband below, but the farmer sat stolidly staring at me across the table as I lay indisposed on the bench, until I grew frantic, and asked him with scant politeness what brought him to travel among these "Islands of the blest." Without any irritation, he replied that two years previously he had had a comparatively large sum of money left him. This he was chiselled out of by relatives and friends (*sic*) until he had only a thousand dollars left, on which he had resolved to travel and see as much for the money as he could. He reckoned he should get some good out of his money that way.

Our provisions fell short. We could with our glasses see the laden breadfruit-trees and coco-palms, the yellow banana clusters, and the natives in gay attire on the narrow beach here and there; but we could not round that point and enter the bay until we had on the fifth day partaken of our last dinner, which consisted of half a potato each, and three sardines among the party.

The captain and his crew had, of course, the never-failing poi, a most nutritious staple food of taro root—*Colocasia antiquorum*—which is cooked, scraped, pounded, fermented slightly, and then mixed with a little water to form a paste, and eaten with the fingers—a most nourishing article of diet, only one needs to get accustomed to it.

But the beauty of that bay and what we saw on Hawaii was worth all the discomforts of the journey, not to mention the wonders of the great volcano. One who was born on the island says: "We dwelt on the arid lava-shores of Kona, below the towering dome of Hualilai, from whose opening sides had, from century to century, gushed black floods of lava, building out the coast into the sea. Some of these broad rock floods seemed still fresh as of yesterday. Inland, where it rained, they were clothed with verdure. The front of our home looked out upon the sea, between the dark tall sinuous stems of coco-palms whose huge yellow fronds swayed far aloft in the cooling sea breeze. From seaward swelled long battalions of mighty rollers, rearing their green crystal fronts, as with combing manes they charged shorewards, to dash in towering spray upon black lava points, or to sweep up the white shell sands of the coves. Down the fronts of these swift combers rode every hour scores of men, women, and children, crouching, lying, and even standing upon their shooting surf-boards, their brown skins gleaming in the sunshine and the foam. Those swarming crowds of gentle, gay, half-naked natives have almost disappeared from these frequented hamlets along the coast. Their cleanly, nicely matted grass cottages, like smooth haystacks, are rarely seen. Spruce white houses of Seattle fir now dot the shores, with here and there a neat little church on a rise of ground. The great double canoes, with the flashing paddle-blades of a score of men, have given place to sloops and whale boats. The lusty brown frames, once girt only with a maro (a loin covering), now saunter in 'store clothes' aping the fashions of the foreigner, although stays still fail of victory over feminine exuberance."

North-west of the island of Hawaii is Maui, with its beautiful valley of Iao, and the great crater of Haleakala (house of the sun) which is, indeed, the largest extinct crater in the world. It is twenty-four miles in circumference, and has walls 2000 feet high. The depth of the crater is 2700 feet. The great Spreckles sugar plantation is on this island, and the soil grows the finest rice that is exported from Hawaii. Coffee too can be grown with advantage, and an intending planter would obtain good land here, rich in phosphates.

Lahaina, the chief town of Maui, is a quiet

A NATIVE GRASS HUT

little place, having one broad street. Formerly a large business was done here with whaling vessels, as many as three hundred having anchored at the same time, but the port is no longer a place of call for foreign trade. Fields of sugar-cane come right down to the town. Pineapples and grapes are grown largely, but years ago vessels used to come here from California for potatoes, flour, and corn. In the early days of the goldfields they did a famous trade with San Francisco.

Landing at Makena, you ascend to Ulupalakua—which name means "ripe breadfruit for the gods," and this is a Paradise for health-seekers; delightfully cool, for it lies 2000 feet above the level of the sea. Corn and potatoes can be grown here, and the cattle are fine and plentiful.

Wailuku is most beautifully situated. It has the lovely Iao Valley at the back, whilst the slopes of the great crater Haleakala stretch before it in front. Wailuku means "the water of slaughter," the valley having been the scene of a battle between the conqueror Kamehameha I. and the King of Maui, when the stream was choked up with dead bodies. Oranges, guavas, limes, and other tropical fruits grow here in profusion, and as to ferns, they are plentiful—from the tree-fern to the most filmy and delicate trauslucent Trichomanes and Hymenophyllum. On the northern side, in deep valleys between the rugged mountains, the rich verdure and exquisite foliage are beyond description; the western slopes again are covered with grass, where the cattle find good pasture. Sugar plantations stretch up the lower part of the north-western slopes of Haleakala, and some of the mountain sides are carpeted with strawberry plants which yield delicious fruit.

Near to Maui are the islands of Lanai and Kahoolawe. From Lanai, Honolulu chiefly draws its supply of mutton; excellent wool is exported to the United States; about fifty thousand sheep graze here, and there are an immense number of wild turkeys. In our time good mutton could be bought at fourpence a pound, and a nice turkey for two shillings, but prices are now higher.

On Lanai is to be seen one of the ancient temples where the cruel rites of the old native religion used to be practised.

Molokai is the island to which all lepers are sent. It is the first of the group sighted on the way from San Francisco to Honolulu. Leprosy broke out first in the islands in 1853, and it spread frightfully during the following ten years. In 1865 an Act was passed by Kamehameha V., ordering the segregation of all those infected, and lands for a leper settlement were obtained on the north side of Molokai. They now have a Protestant, a Roman Catholic, and even a Mormon church, and about 100,000 dollars are spent annually by the Hawaiian Government on the needs of these sufferers, including the education of the children.

Most of my readers will be familiar with the story of the work of Father Damien amongst these unfortunates, and his noble self-sacrifice. Yet I feel bound to speak as to the kindness shown the poor exiles on Molokai by the people of Honolulu themselves. I was living in Honolulu two years before Father Damien's arrival in the islands, and was there also for some time after that, and I was deeply interested in the condition of the people. One writer has said: "Perhaps no spot on the face of the earth could equal, for concentrated misery and hopeless horror, the leper settlement on Molokai."

Yet an Hawaiian on Molokai is in a Paradise

in comparison with some of our own sufferers in England, for he has society and he is in a glorious climate. And the island of Molakai was well looked after in the early days by excellent American missionaries. A Mr. and Mrs. Hitchcock were at the head of the work from 1832 to 1857. They were peculiarly devoted and efficient, and had excellent missionaries associated with them. There were no traders in their field, and their influence was less impeded than on the other islands. Nearly every man and woman on the island came to own their powerful moral and spiritual sway.

But the Roman Catholic members of the community were in the minority, and were certainly neglected, and when the leper settlement was founded, to these especially Father Damien came as a saviour and a brother. He saw what was lacking better than mere visitors could, and, with the help and supplies sent to him, remedied and comforted the poor sufferers. And how bravely!

When my brother-in-law—whose after labours as acting President of the Board of Health, I fear, hastened his death—visited the settlement shortly before the good pastor's death, he held out his hand instinctively in greeting. Father

Damien, with a genial gesture, put his hand behind his back, saying, "It is not the custom to shake hands here."

Happily, leprosy is a disease which numbs sensation, and one of the chief characteristics of these people is an easy-going good temper little given to reflection. At the time I lived in Honolulu there was one woman in Molokai who had been the wife of three lepers in succession, having followed her first husband into exile. She has since died, herself a leper.

All are not, however, resigned to going there. A story is told of a leper who had been condemned to leave his home on the island of Kauai, who took possession of a narrow luxuriant gorge between high mountains, and this he held in possession against the deputy-sheriff and his men. He killed the former, and a large force of militia was then sent to capture him. Three of these he killed, and he forced the rest to quit. For some time he was master of the situation, but at last he was taken.

Whilst I write this, news has come of the murder of Dr. Jared Smith, of Kauai, a man who was locally called "the Beloved Physician," the son of Dr. Smith who formerly practised there. He had declared a woman to be a leper, and her lover, or rather the man who lived with her, shot him. Dr. Smith was shortly to marry, and as he was writing to his betrothed, a knock came at the door; on going to see who the visitor was he was shot dead. Such crimes are rare in Hawaii, but the natives of the island of Kauai have always been notoriously more fierce than those of the other islands, and it has now transpired that the murderer had Malayan blood in him. The late King Kalakaua did infinite harm by selling exemptions to lepers, and even protecting them, against the injunctions of the Board of Health.

The leper lands were given to the Government by a family of chiefs. A clergyman who has devoted some years of his life to the improving of the condition of these poor creatures, says of the settlement: "It is capable of being brought under cultivation, as may be seen from the small orchards of figs, peaches, apricots, and other fruits which are grown there with passable success. This little spot contains a herd of several hundred head of cattle, which furnish both milk and meat for the use of the lepers. The two villages, although somewhat straggling in character, are not without a certain amount of beauty. They are well provided with schools and churches. The most potent cause of death on the island of Molokai is said to be consumption, owing, no doubt, to the cold northerly exposure and the high range of humidity, which makes those susceptible to the disease fall easy victims to it.

" There are at this time at the 'Bishop Home' —a home founded by Mr. C. R. Bishop, formerly a banker of Honolulu, but at present residing in San Francisco—five sisters of the Order of St. Francis, who went there from Syracuse, N.Y., fifteen years ago. These ladies take care of a number of native and other lepers, all females. Besides dressing their loathsome wounds daily, they teach them the ordinary branches taught in schools, and try to impress upon their minds the absolute necessity of personal cleanliness. The same duties are performed at Kalawao by Mr. Joseph Dutton,[*] a man whose name is too little known, for he is one of God's heroes. With him are associated a half-dozen or more lay brothers, who teach

---

[*] Mr. Dutton is a lay brother, a Roman Catholic, a man as devoted as Father Damien. My brother-in-law was struck by the perfect order of all his arrangements: his boys tending the bath-rooms under his direction had all the brasses shining like gold.

boys to look after the general interest of the settlement. A better place for the isolation of this dreadful disease could not have been assigned by Dame Nature herself. An almost inaccessible range of some six thousand feet in height bounds the peninsula on the south, while a rocky, heavily surf-beaten shore forbids the approach of even a small boat unless it is manned by a native seaman.

"In addition to the regular branches taught in all preparatory schools, the men and boys are also taught mechanical trades, such as carpentering, cabinet making, blacksmithing, and other trades. Nothing that can be done is left undone to alleviate their miserable condition." The disease is, of course, not contagious; it is contracted by inoculation. It is much more under control than it used to be, and the large island of Hawaii is reported now as being free of leprosy.

The island of Kauai is termed the Garden Island. Its high lands rise to an altitude of 5000 feet: these are in its centre; near the sea are the cultivated portions, which are irrigated on every side from the hills. It produces far more cane in proportion to its size than any other island, and its rice crop is five

The Eight Inhabited Islands 15

times as large as that of the combined output of the two larger islands of Oahu and Maui. Pleasant houses, surrounded by most luxuriantly growing trees and flowers, are scattered everywhere. Orange groves abound, scenting the air with the fragrance of their blossoms; and roses bloom in profusion on the higher slopes, where it is not quite so hot as nearer the seaboard. The valley of Hanalei is a perfect Paradise. As to the ferns, there is a wealth of them of many varieties; the native girls weave pretty hats with the black glossy stems of the maidenhair. The sandalwood-tree used to grow freely on the island of Kauai, and it was one of the chief sources of revenue to the Hawaiian kings and the high chiefs. Many of the so-called sandalwood boxes are now made of a common light wood scented with "sandalwood oil." Even small bits of the genuine tree, now very rare, retain the scent for very many years.

The first commencement of the sandalwood trade with China was in 1791, when a Captain Kendrick, of Boston, called at Kauai in the sloop *Lady Washington*. He left three sailors behind to collect this, and also pearls, returning again from New England to secure the results.

The chiefs entered readily into the traffic. In speaking of some of these who visited England with Kamehameha II., Mrs. Judd says: "They dress well in fine broadcloth and elegant silks, procured in exchange for sandalwood, which is taken to China and sold at an immense profit; fortunes have been made by certain merchants in this traffic—honourably, of course," she adds satirically, "especially when the hand or foot is used on the scales!"

Some of the chiefs have been made to pay eight hundred and a thousand dollars for mirrors not worth fifty. An uncle of my husband's used to tell us queer stories of this trade. Once, as a very young man, he sailed from San Francisco with a friend; they chartered a little schooner together, and carried a cargo of onions, hoping to return with sandalwood; but as they were long on the voyage the food supplies failed. Life, he declared, was kept in them at last by the green shoots of the onions, which were beginning to sprout; the bulbs themselves they would not eat since this cargo represented all their fortune. The expedition ended in their being wrecked, and they landed penniless in California again. They had merry times, however, in Honolulu, playing whist in the evening, in the light from tallow dips stuck into raw potatoes for lack of candlesticks. That spoke for their comparative sobriety, since an old spirit bottle formed the classical candlestick of those early rovers.

There is a curious phenomenon at Mana in Kauai called "the barking sands." As the foot presses on the sand-banks, a peculiar sound is emitted from them. The grains of sand, on being examined under a microscope, are found to contain tiny cavities; and these tiny hollows cause the barking sound, it is supposed, as the noise is never heard when the sand is wet.

The small island of Niihau lies south-west of Kauai. It has few trees, but the pasturage is excellent, and it looks more familiar in its aspect to the European than other parts of Hawaii. Sheep are raised largely, and cattle in less numbers. The natives cultivate yams plentifully, and they are noted for the mats which they weave of a very fine texture. Their life is less spoilt by foreign contact than is that on the other islands.

Last, but certainly not least, on our list of the eight islands, comes Oahu, on which is the capital of the whole group, Honolulu. Its area is 600 square miles; in agricultural importance it comes fourth on the list, but it possesses the best and, of course, the most frequented harbour. There are two mountain ranges in Oahu; the fertile lands lie in the valleys between the ridges and along the lower spurs, whilst a table-land between the two ranges yields pasturage. The water supply is, however, poorer than on the other islands.

All visitors to Honolulu, even those who only have the few hours during which the Australian steamers remain in harbour, drive up the lovely Nuuanu valley to the Pali, a great precipice 1000 feet above the sea, over which all travellers must pass in crossing the island. It is a seven miles' drive, and generally a delightfully cool one, as the trade winds blow down through the pass. In the early missionaries' days, travellers had to lower themselves down into the valley below by means of iron rods, from hand to hand. Now, however, there is a good road. Kamehameha the Great, coming as conqueror from his own island, drove the King of Oahu up here from the valley below, on to the brink of the precipice, until his followers leaped over in hundreds, to be broken on the rocks beneath. Now there is a good road through.

And what a goodly land is that stretching beyond, on to the lovely blue of the ocean! What marvellous colouring is there! As I looked over it I thought at once of some words of the old hymn :

"So to the Jews old Canaan looked."

The tender green of young rice plants, beyond this coco-palms, and then every tint of the rainbow in the waters.

Nuuanu Valley is lined with beautiful homesteads. Such a wealth of flowering trees and blossoming shrubs is there; all the tropical plants seem at home about a city which has made a Paradise of what was once simply a sandy plain, bare and arid, and treeless save for the fringe of coco-palms along the shore. Even the outbuildings, stables, and wooden sheds are made things of beauty by reason of the masses of brilliant bougainvillia, trailing boughs of the cerise-coloured Mexican creeper, deep-throated purple and white bignonias, and other lovely climbers. The starry blossoms of the stephanotis cover many a verandah. One garden has the magnificent collection of palm avenues planted by Dr. Hillebrand, senior, who was so well known in the botanical world, and whose son is now a great authority on orchids. I paid a delightful visit to him there, and he showed me the many rare and beautiful orchids which he grew, planted in the notches left where old palm-leaves had been cut off. The effect of some of these curiously beautiful bird-like blossoms, hanging down underneath the rich green of the palm-branches, was wonderful. He introduced many valuable tropical plants and shrubs into Hawaii. I treasure still some rare blossoms, not orchids, carefully pressed, that he gathered for me in that rare garden, with my collection of Hawaiian and Tahitian ferns.

As I write of Nuuanu Valley and the slopes above, a singular figure, one that used to pass our cottage often, and to bring herbs and mountain plants for sale, comes before my mind. "Old Oakum" the man was called, on account of his long flowing curly hair, which had grown lighter through exposure to the hot sun. He never wore a head-covering, and his legs from the knee, and his feet, were bare. He always carried a kit, or large grass satchel, hung on a staff over his shoulder, and at least five dogs of all sizes followed always closely at his heels. His kit was filled with mint, which only grew high up in the valley—which we were glad to get as sauce for our lamb or mutton—and rare ferns only to be procured in places that were inaccessible to most. He lived alone in a poor little hut. "Aloha"—"greeting to you"—he would shout at the garden gate, and if I smiled a welcome, in he came and stood under the coffee-tree by my verandah, to yarn away to me about the wonderful spots "only known to himself" in the mountains. One cavern, he told me, was sparkling with precious stones. He said the fairies showed him the way to it.

"And what about your dogs?" I would ask.

"Oh, I make them lie quiet when we get near the place, till I get back to them. I never leave my dogs else, I'm so lonesome without them. They always sleep and never move when I bid them. It is wide and high like a fine church in there, all sparkling with great diamonds."

Poor Oakum! his English was good, and he had a free noble step, in his ragged clothes and bare feet. No one knew his right name. The sailors on the vessel by which he had come, years before, to Honolulu, said that they had heard in "Frisco" that he came as an English gentleman to the Californian gold mines, that whilst there the ground had given way above the spot where he was working. He had been dug out, nearly dead, and had never been right in his mind since: the past was a blank. Down to San Francisco he had drifted, he had managed somehow to get carried to Honolulu, and thenceforth was simply known as Old Oakum. His face, his gait, and his ideas bespoke the gentleman; and his dogs, at any rate, worshipped him.

Old Oakum strides out; and past the gate, down the white coral stone road, under the red-flowering poinsettia trees, sweep a whole bevy of young native women on horseback, with long wreaths of flowers round their necks and round their hats, astride on Mexican saddles, racing and laughing as they gallop down into Honolulu. Some men following hold out, each of them, a long stick upon which are wreaths made of blossoms, closely strung, for sale to the town-dwellers; for no guest at a feast is fully dressed unless he has a garland of flowers round him: even the foreigners like to deck themselves in these. The fragrant Cape jessamine and the wax-like gardenia are in great favour, and a climbing fragrant plant called maile, which is like smilax, only it smells much like our English woodruff.

The women ride most gracefully, albeit astride. Breadths of brightly coloured cloth, sometimes even of satin or velvet, hang down from the waist on either side : this is called a pa-u. Red and yellow are the favourite colours, and the effect of these, when a merry party flashes past, is charming.

What a Paradise the valley above Honolulu seemed to us! Less hot than Tahiti, our last resting-place, its natural beauties were more enjoyable, and it was so much more civilised; "the trail of the serpent" was less visible : the loose immorality of the Society Islands was so flagrant, and had grieved me often, whilst we were amongst an otherwise lovable people there.

On our first visit to Honolulu, we had scarcely been an hour in my sister's charming gabled cottage up the shady valley, when, from various neighbours, smiling native messengers arrived, laden with presents of fruit and cakes and flowers, with congratulations on "the pleasant surprise" to my sister. And she, with her very pretty new bride's frocks fresh from England, was such a goodly sight for my eyes, after five years of absence in New Zealand. I was with her in the lovely garden that same evening, standing to admire the spider lilies and begonias, when I felt suddenly two large soft hands on either shoulder, as though some one were measuring my width, and a native voice—a man's—said, " Like maitai, Jennie maitai loa." This my sister interpreted to be, " Lizzie handsome, Jennie *very* handsome." It was Keoina, the native gardener. The Hawaiians estimate beauty by size. Lean people they do not admire.

The next morning I heard another manly voice call to me from the foot of the stairs, "Your washee ready, Jennie?"

I remonstrated with my sister as to the familiarity of her men servants, but she told me it was the custom of the natives; she had tried to make them say "Mr." and "Mrs.," but they replied, " No, no; too many Smith, too many Judd; you John and Like." They never use the sound of *s*, but substitute *k* for it. One foreign lady, newly arrived, had declared that her servants should never be allowed to address her in so familiar a fashion, and she instructed her husband—she was also a bride—never to mention her Christian name in their hearing.

One day she had some visitors, and, to their great edification, the cook put his head inside the parlour door and asked, "My love, what vegetable you want to-day?" After that she was content to be simply "Mary."

Things are changed now. I am not sure, though, that there is more goodwill and peace in the domestic economy than there was in those primitive days of unvarnished simplicity.

The whole area of the Hawaiian group is about the size of Wales or Saxony. They contain the highest mountains of any island in the world, and only a few of the Alpine peaks are as high as Mauna Loa and Mauna Kea. The climate is much cooler than that of countries in a similar latitude on any of the great continents. This is owing largely to the steady trade winds which come over a great stretch of ocean. Professor A. B. Lyons, the acting director of the Weather Bureau in 1897, wrote from Honolulu on the temperature there, as follows: "It is seldom that the thermometer in Honolulu registers a minimum temperature as low as 55 degrees Fahrenheit. One who is not an early riser will seldom see the mercury below 60. The days in an ordinary year having a mean temperature of less than 70 degrees, or an average for the twenty-four hours as low as 67 degrees, you could count on the fingers of one hand. About as rare is a morning temperature above 76 degrees, or a mid-day maximum in the shade as high as 87 degrees. In sheltered spots, exposed to the full glare of the summer sun the temperature will be a few degrees higher. Only once in the past nine years has there been a maximum of 90 degrees in the shade.

"In my study, with windows open to admit the breeze, the extreme range of the thermometer during three years of continuous observation ranged from 65 degrees to 83 degrees. The maximum daily average of 80 degrees was reached only two or three times in a year, and that in spite of the fact that the room, not a large one, was lighted in the evening by a Rochester lamp. About four days in each year the average temperature was below 70 degrees, once only as low as 68 degrees. Between the middle of April and the middle of December in 1893, the daily average was only twice below 75 degrees and twice above 79 degrees. Is it strange that few houses in Honolulu indulge in the luxury of a fireplace?

"'Equable, yes,' you say, 'but rather

warm.' So it is in Honolulu, and, for that matter, at any point near sea level. But whatever may be said of the possible debilitating effect, on some constitutions, of our perpetual summer, there is little in it to complain of on the score of comfort. The temperature rises by imperceptible gradations from February to August or September. Some days in May and June, before the trade wind settles to its summer pace, suggest the idea that the sun is coming and uncomfortably close, but before many hours the breeze freshens, and you conclude that Nature was merely inviting you to the luxury of a swim in the half-tepid water of the Pacific at Waikiki.

"Warm days are common; they are the rule in September; but there is seldom a suggestion of sultriness in the air. If there is 'muggy' weather at all it is in the cooler part of the year, when the winds are southerly. In summer the dew point is at least 10 degrees lower than the air temperature in the daytime. A sultry night is unheard of. The air always cools sensibly before nightfall, the night temperature being about 10 degrees lower than that of the daytime. If there is little wind the difference is correspondingly greater, the minimum being then occasionally as much as 20 degrees lower than the maximum.

"The first question a prospective immigrant will ask is: Can I work in such a climate? I believe that it is safe to answer in the affirmative, whatever be the character of the work. The danger is that, if you come from a country where the climate prohibits work of certain kinds for days and weeks together, you will over-exert yourself from the instinct to make the most of the present exceptionally favourable opportunity. When you have lived here ten years you may fall into the opposite error of putting off until to-morrow work that can be done as well one day as another.

"In Honolulu through the summer months these trade wind showers, coming at all hours of the day, generally as a mere sprinkle of rain, more numerous and much more heavily freighted in the night, serve to mitigate the tendency to drought, and are sufficient often to keep the grass quite green on the hills. We expect in Honolulu one or two inches of rain a month from these showers.

"When vitality is low and the system needs repose rather than stimulation, a climate subject to no extremes, inviting one continually into the open air, bright but not excessively hot, breezy yet reposeful, is worth crossing an ocean to find. Not a few have experienced its health-restoring power, particularly persons with incipient pulmonary diseases."

CHAPTER II

PLANT LIFE OF THE HAWAIIAN ISLANDS

In a paper written by Professor A. B. Lyons, which he read before a botanical club at the Michigan University, and of which I shall avail myself largely here, he says that: The plants indigenous to this group, may be grouped into about six different floras. Of these, first may be considered the littoral plants, found growing along the seaboard, such as like the salt-impregnated atmosphere and brackish water. These are not, many of them, peculiar to Hawaii. Plants of this group, having generally fleshy stems and leaves, get uprooted often by the waves; they retain their vitality for days and weeks in the sea water, and get re-planted far from the spot on which they first grew. The low coral islets that abound in the Pacific serve as resting-places on their migration. The genus *Scævola* is a marked instance of the littoral species. Extending its range inland, a genus, in adapting itself to new and various environments, will sometimes evolve no less than seven new species.

"The pretty Kipukai is one of this littoral group, found rather on the lava or coral rocks, but always close to the sea. It is a heliotrope; prostrate, wiry stems bear at their upturned ends close rosettes of silky canescent leaves, somewhat suggestive of some of the rock saxifrages." Pure white are the flowers, in small compact clusters.

The Mahukona violet—*Tribulum cistoides*—is another plant which blossoms on sandy or rocky desert-like places near the sea. It has yellow flowers of fragrant scent, but one property it possesses which is less charming. If you should happen—as is often the case in this genial climate—to be exploring barefooted, you will perhaps tread on one of these plants, and then you will jump, and be reminded of the oft-quoted business end of a tin-tack.

Then there is the flora of the low lands, which extends from the sea-shore up to the edge of the forest area. On the nearly bare tufa cone, Diamond Head, or on lava ledges, or old lava flows which have not yet covered themselves with a soil, these plants are to be looked for. There are the *Convolvulaceæ* which drape the lava heaps and make them gay with pink and pale blue blossoms.

Mrs. Francis Sinclair, in a beautiful work which she published on the indigenous flowers of the Hawaiian Islands, says that in olden times, and even within the last fifty or sixty years, great numbers of the natives betook themselves annually to the mountain districts for various purposes, such as canoe-making, bird-catching, gathering medicinal herbs, &c., but that the old healthful industrious life has changed of late years, and it is only from the old people that we can now get reliable information about those plants that grow far from the abodes of the present generation. This sounds bad, but there is much in the fact that they are now many of them engaged in more profitable industries and callings.

The pink convolvulus with darker stripes—*Ipomœa palmata*—when the crops of potatoes and other roots failed, was an article of native diet. The root and the stems were eaten, and the vines, being very strong, were valuable as cordage and much used in house-building, the parts of every well-built dwelling being fastened together with ropes of the ipomœa. The pale blue convolvulus was used for medicinal purposes, stem and roots being pounded into a soft mass which was applied to bruises of all kinds and broken bones. The seeds of the darker red convolvulus—*Ipomœa turpethum*—are used much as a medicine by the natives, and the tiny flowered *Ipomœa batatas*, or sweet potato, which is found nearly all over the world, is used by the natives living on the small island of Nihau, where taro is not grown as the principle means of subsistence. It is a curious fact that these particular natives are especially strong and athletic. The older natives will tell you that nearly fifty varieties of this vine are to be found in their islands. The sweet potato in New Zealand is, of course, an important article of diet. The Maoris have various superstitions connected with it. The tubers must only be planted when the moon is on the increase, and are always planted in the ground lying from north to south.

The *Ipomœa pescapræ*, which grows near the sea, is used by the natives in fishing. They twist the stems into long coils, and with these drive the fish into their nets. The seeds are good as medicine, but if eaten long the root and stems of this variety cause vertigo. The leaves produce the same effect on animals who have eaten them.

The *Capparis Sandwichiana* has large beautiful white flowers with numerous exserted stamens, but when it begins to wither you find the promise it gave of fragrance was deceptive.

Several species of *Hibiscus* with large red and white flowers grow on the margin of the woods, the hau-tree, also a hibiscus with flowers that change from yellow to mauve. This the natives train to cover a rude frame, making a sort of verandah. Such abound outside the dwellings of Waikiki, the pleasant little sea-bathing resort which I describe elsewhere. The milo, a tree which is held sacred in Japan and Tahiti; a species of cotton plant with yellow, and another with red flowers. And then there is a small shrub called Ilima by the natives. Its yellow flowers are worked into leis or garlands, and it might be called the national flower. All these belong to the order of *Malvaceæ*. Probably they were introduced by the aboriginal settlers. The women of the various groups in the Pacific all love to adorn themselves with flowers, and they would in

Plant Life of the Hawaiian Islands

their migrations carry the seeds of such plants as were decorative with them.

In Tahiti, at a large village we once visited, the chief got up a singing festival in our honour. After the music was over, the native performers brought the wreaths they had worn and cast them down at the feet of my husband and myself. It reminded one of the words in Sacred Writ: "Casting their crowns before Him."

Then there is the *Wiliwili* or coral-tree—*Erythrina*—belonging to the forest belt. It is a large thorny tree, having the habit—said to be unique among the native trees—of shedding its leaves completely during the dry season, a proof that the tree has not become completely acclimated. It bears deep red or orange clusters.

The thistle poppy, *Argemone Mexicana*, is perennial in the islands. It has a woody stem, three to six feet high, with very white foliage and large showy white flowers. A very common wild flower this is, but only Hawaiian by adoption. The natives use opium, which they extract from the roots of this poppy, in cases of neuralgia and toothache. The hibiscus will grow here into trees from fifteen to twenty five feet high, cotton-trees ten to fifteen feet, and the coral-tree has often a trunk which is eighteen to twenty-four inches round. Violets in this range, with woody stems, grow from three to eight feet high; raspberries, having canes nearly an inch thick, rise to ten and fifteen feet; and the Ohelo, a whortleberry—Pele's sacred fruit—forms trunks one to two inches in diameter of close-grained wood, and will grow to a height of ten and even fifteen feet.

The lower forest zone may be called the third floral region. It receives rain enough to maintain a continuous growth, but it lies below the line of frequent cloud or mist. The commonest trees are the candle-nut—*Kukui*, in native, signifying light—and the mountain apple or Ohia, a most refreshing fruit to thirsty travellers, though inferior to other apples as an article of food. The Kukui, or candle-nut, is used for making candles, and from it an oil which the natives use in their lamps is extracted. The nuts after lying buried for a period become very like our Whitby jet, and they are carved into earrings and bracelets, &c.

The undergrowth consists of wild ginger in moist places; in the drier spots, of ferns. Foreign plants—such as the lantana, a shrubby vervain, and guava—are crowding out the weaker native plants in this region. Guava-trees in some of the valleys grow from thirty to forty feet high. In the open country it forms a chapparel five to ten feet high. Much jelly is made of the fruit for export, and the pulp is stewed or eaten with sugar as fresh fruit. Guava jelly is said to be valuable in cases of low fever.

The essentially characteristic Hawaiian flora is to be found in the higher forests among the mists and clouds. There are the tree-ferns—*Cibotium* and *Sadleria*—the former having stems five to twelve inches round, and growing from six to twelve or fifteen feet high. Here, too, are the *Rubiaceæ*, *Rutaceæ*, *Araliaceæ*, *Labiatæ*, and *Lobeliaceæ*, which include one-third of the flora which is exclusively Hawaiian; and here also are all the ferns peculiarly Hawaiian. And there is the troublesome climbing pandanus, with ropy stems an inch thick. It is impossible to work one's way through the network of wiry roots which are sent out down the whole length of stem. These fix themselves in the bark of tree trunks, binding the trees together. A growth of the interlaced fronds of the *Gleichenia* ferns again will cover a ridge for miles. Their brown stems are polished, and although not thick, they are so strong that the boys make kite frames of them. As Professor Lyons says, you have to make your way through it by throwing yourself bodily on it to crush it down.

There are two important timber trees on this forest belt: the Koa of the natives, an acacia "whose ordinary foliage consists not of the mimosa-like compound leaves which are seen only on tender shoots of vigorous growth, but of the thick, firm, crescent shaped parallel nerved phyllodes." This Koa is like mahogany; it is used for furniture. Then there is the Lehua, a myrtaceous tree, good for fuel. It grows to a height of thirty to fifty feet, and has tassel-like clusters of crimson, sometimes yellow or orange flowers. The flowers of this region have absolutely no fragrance, although the foliage of the plants is often balsam-like.

The Maile I have referred to elsewhere as being used for wreaths. The myrtle-like leaves retain their scent for many months, and the natives go miles up into the mountains to procure this long, glossy, trailing creeper.

There is a plant that has also a balsam-like odour, somewhat resembling an English ivy, it is called *Olapa*. The resin which exudes from this is used by the natives to perfume their bark cloth, which is called Kapa here, Tapa in Tahiti, a cloth made by beating with infinite pains the bark of trees. In Tahiti, the white Tapa, sacred to the chiefs, may only be beaten out by the young virgins.

The trees in this misty region are covered with wonderful mosses, liverworts, tiny ferns and lycopods. The filmy translucent ferns are lovely here, and the climbing ferns are plentiful.

Parasites, too, such as many of the Aspleniums, the Acrostichums, some small Polypodiums, the grass-like Vittaria, the Bird's Nest fern with its long, bright, glossy fronds, grow on the trunks and in the forks of branches. The wet soil below is not favourable to the growth of the small seeds, the bark of the trees fosters them better.

The flowering plants are nearly all small trees or shrubs; and the tallest Hawaiian tree, with the exception of the coco-nut palm; is not higher than about eighty feet.

There is only one begonia, the *Begonia Hillebrandia*, indigenous to Hawaii. It is a moisture-loving plant and may be found in the ravines where are innumerable waterfalls. There are native Labiatæ, plants of robust growth, half shrubby, with stems of climbing habit. "These differ from ordinary Labiatæ in the fleshy character of the fruitlets."

Most characteristic of all the Hawaiian flora, says Professor Lyons, are the *Lobeliads*, of which there are fifty-eight species; that is, they comprise nearly a tenth of all the flowering plants indigenous in the Hawaiian islands. The family is exceeded in number of species only by that of the *Compositæ*, which has, however, only sixty-one species that do not occur elsewhere. In one species of Lobelia, named Yuccoides, there are racemes two to three feet long, which bear from two hundred to four hundred flowers.

In the higher mountain regions above the cloud belt, where there is frost, there are the interesting arboreus *Compositæ*, "trees whose nerved leaves, tufted at the end of the twigs, suggest anything rather than a relationship with the sunflower or the chrysanthemum."

Then there is the peculiar Silver-sword, growing in the snowy region. This is to Hawaii what edelweiss is to the Alps; you must have gone through much fatigue and perhaps danger, to have it to show. Its stem is several

Plant Life of the Hawaiian Islands

inches round, and it grows some feet high. A head of stiff dagger-like leaves, from eight to twelve inches long, crowns it, and these are covered with a thick glistening white tomentum. On the heights, too, is found a silvery leaved geranium. On the few mountain summits, which are nearly always hidden in the clouds, is a floral area which is unique. Here are to be found bogs covered with grasses, sedges and sphagnum moss, with a number of small plants whose nearest relations are in the mountains of New Zealand, the Southern Andes, and other Antartic regions. The most interesting of these bog plants is a violet.

The breadfruit tree is a beautiful object. Its fruit is much used as a vegetable, but it is somewhat tasteless to Europeans. It is said to have been brought here from Upolu in Samoa. Bananas, yams, taro, the arum succulentum, grow wild in the valleys.

A carefully planted taro patch surrounded by coco-palms is a pretty sight. The long trunks of these palms rise to a height of a hundred feet. The trees begin to bear fruit in the eighth or ninth year, and a full grown palm will bear from one to two hundred nuts annually. Meat and drink, clothing, cooking utensils, oil and canoes, and more can be obtained by the native from his palm-tree. Given the breadfruit, the yam and the coco-nut, with the abundant fish of the tropical islands, and what more does the unspoiled or unsophisticated native need? One day's work a week, up the mountain and on the shore, and he is placed beyond want, and might amuse himself, if he pleased, with surf riding, horse riding, and canoe paddling for the rest of the week.

An American who had married a native, planted a grove of coco-palms with the intention of providing a good income for their daughter, when she should be of age, with the result that she then received from her trees a yearly income of a thousand pounds.

The Papaia is a useful tree. The fruit is like a small pumpkin, yellow. It contains a great quantity of pepsin and may now be bought of our chemists, in a powder, to be taken after meals. In Tahiti all the beef and mutton we ate was wrapped first in a papaia leaf for a few hours to make it tender, as meat cannot, of course, be kept long in a hot climate.

The avocado pear forms a sort of butter to

the breakfast breads; eaten with a little salt and pepper it is delicious. It was imported into Hawaii from Mexico.

I cannot persuade my nieces, who were born in Hawaii, and who, for a time, are now in England, to eat bananas here. After their own beautiful bananas they say they could not touch imported ones, the flavour is so inferior. Mangoes they have, very fine fruit, and several varieties of it.

Pine-apples are grown for exportation. One plantation near Honolulu has a specially delicious kind, one fruit sometimes weighing eight or nine pounds. These fetch high prices in San Francisco.

Oranges, as I have said elsewhere, grow abundantly in some of the higher districts. The flavour of these, especially those from Kono, is delicious. Vancouver gave the first orange trees to Hawaii, with grape vines and other useful plants and seeds.

Hawaii is said to produce more sugar-cane on a given area than any other country in the world, the average product being four tons to the acre, whereas in other countries it is only two to the acre. The seed rarely ripens, so the cane is propagated by cuttings about twelve inches long, taken from below the crown of leaves. The next crop is furnished by the sprouts or suckers after the first crop has been cut.

The sugar-cane is indigenous in Hawaii, but it was little cultivated until a plantation was started on Kauai on land leased by the chiefs in 1835; the methods were then, however, so rough and wasteful that little profit attended its cultivation. In 1895 the value of exports in sugar alone was stated to be £1,595,118, or nearly $8,000,000. The huge rats—a disagreeable importation of the foreigner—have wrought at times much havoc among the canes. To keep these in check the mongous, Lemur mongaz, was introduced. Unfortunately, the mongous found that delicate, plump little game bird, the quail, to be delicious eating, so that the latter threatens to become scarce.

In rice, the value sent to all countries from Hawaii in 1895 was $161,547, or £32,309. This industry is chiefly in the hands of the Chinese, although they do not own the land. From each acre they manage to produce two tons of good, clean rice. The Chinese are the only ones in Hawaii who understand or care to grow rice. But do not these patient and industrious people generally do the unpleasantest and hardest work in those countries where they are welcomed as immigrants? The body of a Chinaman is said to lie beneath every sleeper of the railroad line across the Isthmus of Panama. Let us give him his due.

Chinese buffaloes, described as a half cow, half pig, toil along, with a rough sort of wooden plough to turn up the soil, and the crop is gathered in by the Chinamen with small hand-sickles. When the rice has been bundled up, after a day's hot sun on it, it is carried on the shoulder, two bales on a stick, patient John Chinaman trotting off with it, cheerfully, if apparently, stolid, to be threshed, perhaps a quarter of a mile away.

Much of the soil that is unfit for rice or sugar will bear coffee well. Fortunately the natives take to this industry, and what they produce in Kona, on the island of Hawaii, where the natives work in it largely, is exceedingly fine in flavour. The value of its export in 1895 was $22,823, or £5564 odd.

Tea planting has been tried in Hawaii, but without success.

Although foreign enterprise and capital have accomplished great things in developing the resources of Hawaii, the Hawaiians themselves have benefited greatly; and President Dole, himself the son of one of the early missionaries, worked for many years, before he became President, to bring about an efficient homestead purchase system, which has enabled the natives, many of them, to purchase tracts of Government land on easy terms. In 1893 he said: "It is a matter of rapidly growing sentiment in the Hawaiian community that a liberal policy of opening for settlement suitable portions of the public lands, by actual occupiers, has become a necessity to the social and industrial progress of our varied population. It is the desire of the executive, if circumstances permit, to inagurate a comprehensive policy of opening public land for settlement and cultivation in answer to the public demand"—(the demand was for land in small parcels for cultivation and residence)—"which, without interfering with established industrial enterprises, may lay the foundation for individual welfare and contentment, and therefore of enhanced public prosperity."

So far from its being the sons of missionaries who desire to take the land from the native Kanakas, I found *always*, in my observations whilst in Hawaii, that those who had been born there had an affection for the people and sought to promote their welfare.

The proportion of native Hawaiians holding real estate is now really very large. It had increased in six years—that is, from 1890 to 1896—22 per cent., although during the same period that class of the population had decreased 10 per cent. In the same time the *part-native* owners actually increased 83 per cent., while their own numbers had increased 37 per cent.

The Portuguese, who, when they first came, were chiefly labourers, had in six years increased their real estate holdings 87 per cent. They thrive greatly in Hawaii, and have multiplied 76 per cent. in the same time. Most of the dairy farming is carried on by them, and the rearing of goats. They bring their wives with them in immigrating, and are a thrifty and industrious race as a rule.

The holdings of the native people are small ones, but these have been much increased of late years. The great bulk of valuable land is certainly owned by white people, who bought it from the Government, or else from the large estates of former high chiefs who left few heirs.

There are now two or three Mormon settlements in Hawaii, one of these, Laie, being on the same island as Honolulu. I remember well my husband bringing me the news of the arrival of the first party of these from the Salt Lake Valley. John Brigham Young, one of the chief elder Brigham Young's numerous sons, was in charge of the immigrants, a fine-looking young man. In Hawaii they are well respected. Of course, they have only one wife; the law of the land in any case would forbid a plurality of these. Many go round the islands as missionaries, and converts have land given to them rent free as well as assistance in building their houses.

CHAPTER III

ORIGIN OF THE HAWAIIANS: THEIR EARLY CUSTOMS AND RITES

PROFESSOR ALEXANDER, who is the best authority on the history of the Hawaiian race, considers that the question of its origin has not yet been fully solved.

The Polynesian race includes all the natives of the groups of islands in the Eastern Pacific from New Zealand to Hawaii, and including Easter Island. Their languages have much in common, the differences being only a point of dialect; their customs and manners are closely alike; the tabu system obtained in all, and their traditions are the same.

The people of the Malay Archipelago, again, resemble these people greatly: they are all brown-skinned, with long, smooth, if curly hair; and some authorities believe that the Polynesians came originally from the south-west of Asia. In Tahiti I have met men who affirmed that the Tahitians were originally Jews, and I confess that I noted among them many peculiarities of customs and physical traits that might lead to this conclusion.

The Maoris say that their ancestors came from Hawaiki, which is only a variation of the word Hawaii.

According to the Hawaiian traditions, Wakea —who in the Marquesas and Hervey Islands is the God of light—with his wife Papa, were the founders of the race of their chiefs. They are said to have inaugurated the tabu system. During the period that followed their visit, there are said to have been many great works carried out, such as the building of heiaus— places of sacrifice—and the construction of great fishponds in some districts. Besides these there are ancient works which have been a source of much conjecture, but which tradition says were carried out by the *Menehune* people, a race of industrious elves or dwarfs. During the eleventh and twelfth centuries after Christ there seems to have been much enterprise and movement. The Hervey Islands and New Zealand were then colonised, according to local tradition.

Then also it is said that Paao, a priest from Upolu in the Samoan Islands, came with a retinue of followers to Hawaii, where he was made high priest, and he built the great heiau of Mookini in Kohala. The last high priest in his direct line was Hewahewa, who officiated in the reign of the first Kamehameha. It is said that he found Hawaii without a king, on account of the crimes of the chief of Hawaii, and that he returned to Kahiki—which word is used always to indicate any foreign country— and brought back a chief whom he made king. This king, Pili, is said to have been the direct ancestor of the Kamehamehas.

A great navigator of this time was Kaulu, who visited many islands in the company of a foreign astronomer and famous voyager from the south. President Dole, the head of the Hawaiian Republic, translated some of the native song of Kaulu ; here is a portion of it :

> "I am Kaulu,
> The adopted son of Kalona,
> The far-seeing explorer,
> Who forbiddeth sleep,
> Who watcheth for the daybreak,
> Who hurleth the spear.
> Kaulu of the land! Kaulu of the sea!
> O Kaulu, the builder of canoes!

> O Kaulu, the pilot of the fleet!
> Thou spannest the heavens;
> Thou canst grasp the night and the day;
> Thou canst reach out to the ends of the earth;
> All lands are explored by Kaulu.

Then there was another chief of Oahu called Paumakua who was renowned as a navigator. He went south, and brought back with him several priests "foreigners, or *haoles*, of large stature, light complexion, and bright saucy eyes, from whom several priestly families on Oahu claim descent." Other long voyages also are told of in old Hawaiian song, of one who introduced the use of the great drum which was covered with a shark's skin, to the great admiration and wonder of the Hawaiians. From him the chiefs of Oahu and Kauai were descended. He himself returned to Kahiki, which name, though used for any foreign part, is palpably Tahiti. He sailed from the west end of the island of Kahoolawe, which is still named *Ke-ala-i-Kahiki*—the way to Tahiti. During this period of frequent voyages there was a great increase in the influence of priestcraft and in the power of the tabu, also in the frequency of human sacrifices. In the following generation there was less intercourse with the

The Origin of the Hawaiians 53

islands to the south, but the influence of these enterprising navigators is seen stretching on for some hundreds of years.

There is now living in Honolulu an accomplished native lady, Mrs. Emma Nakuina. She is a notary public, practising there. Highly cultivated and well read in European history, she has herself written about the songs and traditions of her own people. A legend of Oahunui, told by this lady, will be of interest here. I have only made one or two verbal alterations in the narrative.

"On the plateau or table-land lying between Ewa and Waialua on the island of Oahu, and about a mile off the present Kaukonahua bridge, is the historical place of Kukaniloko.

"This was the ancient birthplace of the Oahu kings and rulers. It was incumbent on all women of the royal line to retire to this place when about to give birth to a child, on pain of forfeiting the rank, privileges, and prerogatives for her expected offspring, should that event happen in a less sacred place.

"The stones were still standing ten years ago, and maybe are yet undisturbed, where the royal accouchements took place. In ancient times this locality was tabu ground, for here the high priest of the island had his headquarters. In some matters his authority was paramount to that of the king.

"A few miles from Kukaniloko, towards the Waimea Mountains, is Halemano, where the last of the cannibal chiefs from the South Seas finally settled when they were driven from the plains of Mokuleia and Waialua by the enraged people of those districts, who were exasperated by the frequent requisitions on the original inhabitants by the stranger chiefs in order to furnish material for their cannibal feasts.

"To the east of Halemano and about the same distance from Kukaniloko is Oahunui (Greater Oahu), another historical place. This was the residence of the kings of the island. Tradition has it that previous to the advent of the cannibal strangers this place was known by another name.

"When the Lo-Aikanaka, as the last of the man-eating chiefs are called in history, were constrained to take up their residences in Upper Halemano, a district just outside of the boundaries of those reserved for the royal and priestly residences, a young man called Oahunui was king. An elder sister called Kilikiliula, who had been as a mother to him, was supposed to share equally with him the

The Origin of the Hawaiians

royal power and prerogative. This sister was married to a chief named Lehuanui, one of the priestly line, but not otherwise directly connected with royalty, and she was the mother of three children, the two oldest being boys and the youngest a girl. They all lived together in the royal enclosure, but, according to ancient custom, in separate houses.

"Now the Lo-Aikanaka, on establishing themselves in Upper Halemano, had at first behaved very well. They had been circumspect and prudent in their intercourse with the royal retainers, and had visited the young king, to whom they rendered their homage with every appearance of humility.

"Oahunui was quite captivated by the plausible, suave manners of the ingratiating southern chief and his immediate retainers, and he invited them to a feast. This civility was reciprocated, and the king dined with the strangers. Here, it was strongly suspected that the dish of honour placed before the king was human flesh served under the guise of pork.

"The king found the dish very much to his liking, and intimated to the Lo-Aikanaka chief that his cook understood the preparation and cooking of pork better than the royal cook did.

"The Lo-Aikanaka chief took the hint, and the young king became a very frequent guest of the Southerners. Some excuse or other to invite the royal guest would be such as a challenge to the king to a game of konane, or a contest of skill in the different athletic and warlike sports would be arranged, and Oahunui would be asked to be the judge or simply invited to view them. As a matter of course, it would be expected that the king would remain after the sports and partake of food when on friendly visits of this nature. Thus, with one excuse or another, he spent a great deal of his time with his new subjects and friends.

"To supply the particular dainty craved by the royal visitor, the Lo-Aikanaka had to send out warriors to the passes leading to Waianae from Lihue and Kalena, and also to the lonely pathway leading up to Kalaikini on the Waimea side, there to lie in ambush for any lone traveller or belated single person in quest of flowers or ferns. Such a one would fall an easy prey to the Lo's stalwart men.

"This went on for some time, until the unaccountable disappearance of so many people began to be connected with these frequent entertainments by the southern chiefs. Oahunui's subjects began to hint that their young king had acquired the taste for human flesh at these feasts, and that it was to gratify his unnatural appetite for the horrid dish which caused his frequent visits, contrary to all royal precedents, to those who were his inferiors.

"The disapproval of his people of the intimacy of Oahunui with his new friends was expressed more and more openly, and murmurs of discontent grew loud and deep. His chiefs and the high priests became alarmed, and begged him to discontinue his visits, or they would not be answerable for the consequences. The king was thereby forced to heed their admonitions, and he promised to stay away from the Los. For a time he kept his word.

"Now all the male members of the royal family ate their meals with the king when he was at home. These included, among others, Lehuanui, his sister's husband, and their two sons, healthy, chubby little lads of about eight and six years of age. One day after breakfast, as the roar of the surf at Waialua could be distinctly heard, the king remarked that the fish of Ukoa pond, at Waialua, must be pressing on to the floodgates, and he would like some aholehole. This observation really meant a command to his brother-in-law to go and get the fish, as he was the highest chief present except his two royal nephews, who were too small to assume such duties.

"Lehuanui, Kilikiliula's husband, accordingly went to Waialua with a few of his own family retainers and a number of those belonging to the king. They found the fish packed thick at the gates, and were soon busily engaged in scooping out, cleaning, and sorting them. It was quite late at night when Lehuanui, fatigued with the labours of the day, lay down to rest. He had been asleep but a short while when he seemed to see his two sons standing by his head. The eldest said to him: "Why do you sleep, my father? While you are down here we are being eaten by your brother-in-law the king. We were cooked and eaten, and our skulls are now hanging in a net from a branch of the lehua-tree you are called after, and the rest of our bones are tied in a bundle and buried under the tree by the big root running to the setting sun."

"Then they seemed to fade away, and Lehuanui started up, shivering with fear. He hardly knew whether he had been dreaming or had actually seen an apparition of his little sons. He had no doubt they were dead, and as he remembered all the talk and innuendoes about the king's supposed reasons for visiting the strangers and the enforced cessation of those visits at the urgent request of the high priest and the chiefs, he came to the conclusion that the king had only expressed a desire for fish in his presence in order to send him out of the way. He reasoned that no doubt the king had noticed the chubby form and rounded limbs of the little lads, and being debarred from partaking surreptitiously of human flesh, had compelled his servants to kill, cook, and serve up his own nephews. In satisfying his depraved appetite, he also got rid of two who might become formidable rivals, for it was quite within the possibilities that the priests and chiefs in the near future, should he be suspected of further cannibalism, might depose him, and proclaim either one of the young nephews as his successor.

"The father was so troubled that he aroused his chief body servant, and the two left Waialua for home shortly after midnight. They arrived at the royal enclosure at dawn, and went first to the lehua-tree spoken of by the apparition of the child, and on looking up amid the branches, sure enough there were hung two little skulls in a piece of large-meshed fishing net. Lehuanui then stooped down and scraped away the leaves and loose dirt from the root indicated, and out rolled a bundle of tapa—native cloth—which on being opened was found to contain the bones of two children. The father reached up for the net containing the skulls, and putting the bundle of tapa in it, tied the net round his neck. The servant stood by, the silent and grieved spectator of a scene whose meaning he fully understood.

"The father procured a stone adze, and went to the king's sleeping-house, the servant still following. Here every one but an old woman tending the kukui-nut candle was asleep. Oahunui was stretched out on a pile of soft mats covered with his paiula, the royal red cloth of old. The cruel monster had eaten to excess of the hateful dish he craved, and having taken also copious draughts of awa juice, he was in a heavy drunken sleep.

"Lehuanui stood over him, adze in hand, and called: "O king, where are my children?" The stupefied king only stirred uneasily: he would not or could not awake. Lehuanui called him three times, and the sight of the drunken brute, gorged with his own flesh and blood, so enraged the father that he struck at Oahunui's neck with the stone adze he held, and severed the head from the body at one blow.

"The father and husband then strode to his own sleeping-house, where his wife lay asleep with their youngest child in her arms. He aroused her and asked for his boys. The mother could only weep without answering. He upbraided her for her devotion to her brother and for tamely surrendering her children to satisfy the appetite of the inhuman monster. He reminded her that she had equal power with her brother, that the latter was very unpopular, and had she chosen to resist his demands and called on the retainers to defend her children, the king would have been killed and her children saved.

"He then informed her that as she had given up his children to be killed for her brother, he had killed the latter, and crying, "You have preferred your brother to me and mine, you will see no more of me and mine," he tore the sleeping child from her arms and turned to leave the house.

"The poor wife and mother followed, and flinging herself on her husband, attempted to detain him by clinging to his knees; but the father, crazed by his loss and the thought that she had greater affection for a cruel inhuman brother than for her own children, struck at her with all his might, exclaiming, 'Well, then, follow your brother!' Then he rushed away, followed by all his retainers.

"Kilikiliula fell on the side of the stream opposite to where the lehua-tree stood, and she is said to have turned to stone, which is pointed out to this day, balanced on the side hill of the ravine formed by the stream. It is one of the sights for the Hawaiian travellers.

"The headless body of Oahunui lay where he was killed, abandoned by every one. The story runs that in process of time it also was turned to stone as a witness of the anger of the gods and their detestation of his horrible crime, and the place was ever afterwards known as Oahunui. All the servants who had in any way been concerned, in obedience to the royal mandate, in killing and cooking the young princes, were, at the death of Kilikiliula, likewise turned to stone, just as they were, in the various attitudes of crouching, kneeling, and sitting.

"The rest of the royal retainers, with the lesser chiefs and guards, fled in fear and disgust from the place, and thus the once sacred royal home of the Oahuan chiefs was abandoned and deserted.

"The ban of the great god Kane's curse, it is believed, still hangs over the desolate spot, in proof of which it is asserted that, although all this happened many hundreds of years ago, no one has ever lived there since."

In old times the Hawaiian people comprised three distinct classes. First came the Alii or nobility, which included the kings of the different islands, and the chiefs, who were of various degrees of rank. The priests, or Kahuna, formed the second class, and this included priests, sorcerers, and doctors. Third came the Makaainana, or labouring class, all the common people. One of these could never rise to be a chief, nor could a chief be degraded; he might be killed or offered as a human sacrifice to the gods, a common fate if vanquished in battle.

As it was believed that the chiefs descended from the gods, they were regarded as sacred; and after his death a chief took his seat among the gods and was worshipped as such. There was—and still is, generally—a great difference between the appearance and bearing of one of the nobility and one of the common people. In Tahiti, and no doubt also here, there were certain foods, always most nourishing ones, which were sacred to the use of the nobility. In person these were always far finer and of greater stature. The chiefs only might wear the red feather cloak or helmet and an ivory clasp, which was called *niho palaoa;* their canoes were painted a red colour; and they were attended by men bearing kahilis, the long sticks with feathered tops of which I say more hereafter.

When the highest chiefs appeared, the common people prostrated themselves on the ground before them; certain of these only went abroad at night.

If the king's name was mentioned, even in song, it was death to remain standing; or even when his food or clothing was carried by. No one might enter his enclosure, cross his shadow or even that of his house. A common man had to crawl into his king's presence, indeed he might never stand erect in audience before him. To touch the head of the king was treason, and if the king was in the cabin of a vessel no subject might show on deck.

The use of the kahili was to blow flies away from the sacred person. Another attendant took care of the spittoon, whilst a third always was at hand to *lomi-lomi*, *i.e.*, to shampoo and knead the royal personage when required. This is still a universal practice among the white as well as the native people. In Tahiti, too, a traveller, on entering a house, is always given a mat to lie on, and his weary limbs are shampooed whilst food is prepared for him.

A great chief had also a following of priests, magicians or diviners, bards and story-tellers, not to mention the dancers, drummers, and jesters. These were called the *aialo*, *i.e.*, those who eat in his presence. His chief attendants were, as a rule, a class who were only noble on the father's side.

The chiefs owned most of the soil and its produce, the fish of the sea and the labour of the people. The system was closely allied to our own early feudal system, but there were some restraints on this arbitrary condition of things: a man might, if he chose, leave one chief for the service of another, so, as a rule, tenants were treated with a certain amount of consideration.

If a chief died all his estates went to his king.

In case of theft, or some other crimes, the offended one avenged himself, if strong enough, or he called in the help of the sorcerer, or failing this, got help from his chief, whose executioner often did his work when the offender was asleep.

The influence of the priests was very great indeed; lands were set apart for their support; and with them lay the power to select human victims for sacrifice. They were the instructors of the nation, and the long prayers which formed part of the religious ceremonies were taught by them to the children. They were the *savants*—the art of medicine, the history of the islands, astronomy, all were in their keeping; and a knowledge of the stars was of the very highest importance, since the navigators found their way on the sea, out of sight of land, through their aid. A navigator would, oftener than not, take an astronomer with him. The diviners and the sorcerers, who prayed people to death—and this is a form of witchcraft still practised in secret—and those doctors who

The Origin of the Hawaiians 67

performed cures by charms and incantations were a lower class of the same priesthood.

Below the common people were the bond-slaves, probably prisoners of war. These were marked on the forehead.

The first man killed in any battle was called a *lehua* and he was always offered in sacrifice. Idols were carried in the ranks, and the priests accompanied the combatants to excite them and also to terrify the enemy by their horrible yells and gestures. Their weapons consisted of long spears, javelins, daggers, and clubs made of a very hard wood.

When Captain Vancouver visited Hawaii in 1793, he presented Kamehameha I. with a bull and a cow, the first of these cattle seen in the islands. Kamehameha then made a state visit to Vancouver, in feather cloak and helmet, with a suite of eleven double canoes, and he presented the captain with four feather helmets, ninety hogs, and a quantity of fruit and vegetables. Vancouver was of more generous fibre than Captain Cook : he gave all the live stock he had left in return, a showy scarlet cloak to the king, and liberal gifts to his followers.

Kamehameha then displayed his skill in spear exercise; he got up a sham battle among one hundred and fifty of his warriors, and when six spears were cast at the same time at his royal person, he caught three, parried two, and dexterously avoided the sixth.

They had some natural fortresses which they improved on; but it was John Young, Queen Emma's maternal ancestor, of whom I tell later, the English sailor detained by Kamehameha from a fur-trader, who had charge of the king's cannons in 1795. He was made Governor of Hawaii, and in 1816 a fort to command the harbour was constructed at Honolulu under his direction.

Cannibalism was never practised by the true, native Hawaiians.

Offers of marriage came as often from the women as from the men, but, as rank, amongst them, was always transmitted through the mother, the marriage of the chiefs was a matter of strict care; sometimes this led, however, to the intermarrying of brothers and sisters.

King Lunalilo's mother, who died only in 1845, was married to the first Kamehameha, although he had been her mother's husband; and when he died she was wife to his son Kamehameha the Second. Yet she was a fine character, a true Christian in her later years, and she gave one-tenth of her income to religious purposes. The American mission teachers kept her closely at study for many hours every day, and she proved a grateful pupil. Formerly she had been the chief repository of Hawaiian lore, having a most retentive memory for legends, songs, and ancient proverbs. Kekauluohi was her name; she deserves to be remembered in the history of her people. Had it not been for the love of strong drink, her son, Prince William—Lunalilo—might have had a long and useful reign.

An amusing instance of broken traditions occurred when Kamehameha's pew in the first Christian church was being arranged. As it was not etiquette for any one to sit above the king, and yet the seats in the galleries in the church were to be filled by the common people, there was strong feeling among some of the old chiefs and their retainers. The sensible king soon settled the question. "I prefer a place near the pulpit and to have fresh air by a window," he said; "I do not care who is in the galleries, if they do not break through."

So a pleasant cushioned pew was arranged

to his royal liking, and the window was draped with orange and crimson satin.

With all their vaunted, easy, good nature, children were often put to death—of this I tell more fully hereafter—and the girls were more often put to death than the boys. The old people were despised and neglected in the lowest caste, and the mad were stoned to death sometimes. Kamehameha, however, did his best to improve the public feeling in this direction, and he issued this proclamation: "Old men and old women shall pass and lie down in safety on the road."

One class of the old Hawaiian deities was composed of the spirits of departed great ones, besides which there were some spirits that haunted certain localities, lonely and dangerous spots, who had to be propitiated. Some watched over the families of the chiefs, and others presided over the different trades. The shark gods, for instance, were worshipped by fishermen, because the shark was supposed to be the embodiment of a malicious spirit. The lizard gods were resorted to by necromancers. The Hawaiians, indeed, believed that earth, air and sea were filled with invisible beings, some malicious, others beneficent; these they called

The Origin of the Hawaiians

akuas. There were also little elves who lived in the woods. In Tonga, until the present century, was shown the hook of Maui, one of the demi-gods, who were men gifted with supernatural powers. Maui was said to be able to obtain fire for men, to draw up islands from the bottom of the sea, to hold back the sun so that day was lengthened at his will. He was celebrated throughout Polynesia for the wonders he wrought with that hook. Of Pele, the goddess of volcanoes, I tell in a separate chapter. The owl was a sacred bird; if seen in times of danger it was considered a good omen. A legend is told of a prisoner of war who was tied up for roasting, but was set free by his guardian god, an owl.

But the four great gods—four was a somewhat sacred number always with these people—were Kane, Kanaloa, Ku, and Lono, and these were supposed to have been co-existent with light. Kane—Tane, in the Society Islands—was the father of men and the founder of this earth. He was more noble than the other gods. Kanaloa was his brother; he was the creator of water-springs, and he brought, they said, trees and fruits from Tahiti to Hawaii. Ku was an evil god who delighted in human sacrifice and other cruelties. New Year games were held in honour of the pleasant god Lono, but the temples and tabus of Ku were held in greater awe than those of Lono.* In 1807 the wife of the great Kamehameha becoming very ill, a priest declared that the gods were angry because certain men had eaten tabu coco-nuts, hence the danger to the queen's life. Ten men were seized as victims by order of the king, but as the dangerous symptoms abated, only three or four of these were slain and offered in the temple at the foot of Diamond Head, near Honolulu.

There were sanctuaries in which, in time of war, men could be in perfect safety, and to one of these a man who had violated a tabu, a thief, or even a murderer, could flee and be preserved. On entering, he had to offer a short formal thanksgiving to the idol. In war time a white flag on the top of a tall spear marked the entrance to these sacred enclosures, and any one trying to follow or injure one who had claimed protection was immediately put to death by the priest's orders. One of the temples near Honolulu was sacred also to the sick.

* It was this god Lono who was at first supposed to be embodied in the person of Captain Cook.

The tabu system is said to have been more perfected in Hawaii than in any other islands of Polynesia. It was tabu for men and women to eat together; they might not even use the same oven. The chapel for the family idols and the men's eating-house might not be entered by the women under penalty of death. Bananas, coco-nuts, pork, turtles, and certain kinds of fish were forbidden to women. Was this due to innate selfishness in men I wonder, for these are the foods most prized; or was the thought, "lest they become as men"? Death was the punishment for breaking this tabu.

The services in the temple were very elaborate. The many prayers had been handed down for generations. During some of these perfect silence was enjoined, as they supposed that any noise would break the charm. At given signals, during some prayers, the congregation would rise and hold their hands toward heaven for a given time—half an hour often. The supreme act of their worship was the human sacrifice; these victims, as above stated, were prisoners in time of war or breakers of the tabu. Women do not seem to have been offered up in sacrifice, and one or more of the male sex have suffered at times in their stead in case of broken tabu—one compensation, at any rate, for their enforced abstinence from good things.

There were many ceremonial observances most interesting to the student of the religions of the world. Space forbids our entering into these here, but in reading of them it would seem as though the Hawaiian people had a more interesting individuality than that of the other races in the South Pacific. They were ever more hospitable than most. In their daily ritual, the Samoan head of his family would pray to his household gods, when the fire was kindled before the evening meal, " Drive away from us sailing gods, lest they bring disease and death"; but the Hawaiians gave ever a gracious welcome to the stranger.

I may repeat here a story that I told in a little book which I published twenty years ago on the child life of Hawaii.

A traveller who visited the islands in the early days, soon after the people had begun to be taught, told an old friend of mine that, having heard that the people had many savage customs, he thought it necessary to be well armed and on the alert in some of the more lonely parts of the country. During his first journey, he stopped one night to sleep in the hut of a native who offered him hospitality. Just as he was falling asleep, after a time of uneasy fears, quiet, stealthy steps approached his mat, and he thought some murderous attack was about to be made. Pretending to be asleep, his senses were all on the alert. The native stood over him for a moment, then, apparently convinced that he was sleeping, moved away; on which the traveller opened his eyes, and watched the man with great anxiety as he took something out of a chest. He made sure that murder was planned. His host, however, took simply a book in his hand, sat down to read, and then, kneeling down, prayed with earnest gestures. The visitor then sat up and asked what he was saying; to which the native replied that he was praying God to bless the stranger who had come to his hut!

Devotional feeling is innate in the Hawaiian. A fisherman might never use a new net or rod without prayer or sacrifice. When a male child was born, he was always taken to the temple; offerings were made and prayers said by the priests, after these the father prayed to the four great gods to grant his son a long and prosperous life. When the boy was four or five years old, he was removed from the common sleeping house to the men's eating house, where he might begin to eat the foods that were tabu to women. But first a hog, bananas and coconuts were offered to the gods before the assembled congregation, and the father had to recite a long prayer. The same rites were performed at the feast of circumcision.

The minds of the masses were, however, much more influenced by the spells of magicians and sorcerers than by the services in their temples, and the effect was debasing. Professor Alexander writes that the practices of a class of these sorcerers "strongly resembled those of modern spiritism. The medium was called the *kahu*, or *ipu*, of the spirit, which was often called a *makani* or wind. Sometimes the spirit descended upon the *kahu*, and sometimes it spoke from the roof of the hut. The necromancer always demanded *awa*—a native drink, which is prepared by chewing the roots of a plant, spitting the mess out into a bowl, and pouring water on this—before commencing operations. After drinking the *awa*, the wind descended upon the *kahuna*, and showed him the cause of the sickness, whether the patient had been bewitched by a sorcerer, and by whom. The same practitioners were employed in cases of theft, to recover stolen goods and to detect the thief."

To effect the purposes of sorcery it was necessary to secure some object connected with the person to be acted on. So the chiefs always had faithful attendants at hand who religiously burned, or buried, or sank out at sea the parings of his nails, the hair cut off, the contents of the spittoon, &c. Fortune-telling was then, as now in civilised countries, a most profitable calling, so was the interpreting of dreams. A curious belief was that each person had two souls, one of which could leave the body in dreams, trances, &c. So if a diviner told his neighbour, as he often did, that he had seen his double or wraith in a vision, wandering naked, with his eyes shut and tongue hanging out, the victim was in danger, and would do or give anything that the diviner required.

The spell exercised by dreams is very curious, and will, it would seem, always have a hold on mankind. The idea of the tongue hanging out, in a dream, being a sign of great evil, or ruin, is still held to by some of our own people.

The astrologers were a better class, and it was they who kept up the knowledge of the stars which the old navigators possessed. They studied the heavens continually, and the positions of the moon and planets in relation to fixed stars and certain constellations, regulated their predictions, as these were supposed to be the ruling influences over the fortunes of certain high families. From signs in the sky, tidal waves, the appearance of shoals of particular fish and other natural phenomena, some soothsayers also predicted the deaths of chiefs and other national events.

Attached to the high chiefs were also prophets called kaula ; these were harmless fanatics of solitary habits, who believed themselves to be inspired by a deity who gave his attention solely to this office.

When a king died, a human sacrifice was made, so that one of his rank might not enter another world without suitable attendance. Their notions of a future state were, however, most crude and contradictory. Some dirges tell that a deity, whose long name signifies "the eyeball of the sun," conducts the souls of heroes to a heaven in or above the clouds. Other traditions say they go to the father God Kane,

The Origin of the Hawaiians

to his hidden land in the west. This is said to be a beautiful island, full of coco-nut trees, which appeared from time to time, like a mirage, to the eyes of mariners. The common belief was that most of the dead haunted their place of sepulture for a few days, trying to destroy or injure their enemies; but they grew weaker every day, and soon they went to an underground sort of Hades.

There is a myth about a hero named Hiku, who descended by means of a long rope, made of convolvulus vines, into the abyss of Milu in order to bring back from thence his bride Kawelu. The Maoris have a similar legend. Certainly these must have an Eastern origin. Milu was said to have been an ancient chief of very evil life, who became king of an abode of misery and darkness, where were streams of water, but the only solid food consisted of butterflies and lizards.

The cutting tools of the Hawaiians were made of stone, sharks' teeth or bamboo; the axes were formed of a hard close kind of lava obtained from the summits of the craters of Mauna Kea and Haleakala. The art of making these was handed down from father to son;

and with their rough implements they managed to carry on some very extensive works.

They have many artificial fishponds, of which there are none in the islands of Southern Polynesia. Their canoes were hollowed out of a single tree, and steadied by an outrigger. The double canoes were from fifty to a hundred feet long, having a raised part in the middle which was for chiefs and persons of high rank. The sails were made of mats. The kukui-nut candles, to which I refer elsewhere, were made by baking the nuts in an oven; then the kernels are strung on a bit of bamboo or the thin stem of a coco-nut leaf. One nut would burn only a few minutes but it would set fire to the nut below it, and then the burned out nut was broken off. The kukui is the *Aleurites moluccana*. Its oil, as well as fish oil, was also burned in stone lamps

The Hawaiians had many games but they were most of them associated with gambling; betting prevailed to a very large extent. Boxing was the favourite national sport; wrestling and running matches were also much in favour. Sledge racing was very popular. A smooth track was made down a steep hillside and then covered with dry grass. Grasping his sledge

The Origin of the Hawaiians

about the middle with the right hand, the actor ran a few yards, then threw himself with all his force on to the sledge, and shot down the hill head-foremost. Surf-riding on boards is still much practised. An ancient amusement was to leap from a great height into the water. They would swing, too, on a long rope fastened to a high coco-nut palm or skip with a rope as our children do. An odd game played only by the chiefs was shooting mice with bow and arrows. Cock-fighting also they were addicted to. The children had games much like our own, even a cat's-cradle sort of game which they played with strings.

Their musical instruments were very simple and the dancing—hula-hula, the national dance is called—was more an acting in gestures, rather an illustration of the ideas in the songs which they accompanied, than true dancing. The dance songs were mostly inspired by the baser sentiments and instincts. The women wore wreaths of flowers on the head and over neck and body, dogs' teeth buskins on the ankles and hogs' teeth bracelets on the wrists with a whale's tooth ornament on the neck. The influence of the hula-hula was degrading. Sometimes large companies of women formed a solid square, and danced in time, that is, they moved arms and body in keeping with the subject of the song.

They were always passionately fond of their poetry, which took the form of short musical lines, attention being given to the accent or rhythm of the last word; there was no rhyming or regular metre. They had poems in the form of religious chants—prayer or prophecy; name-songs which were composed at the birth of a chief, telling of the heroic deeds of his forefathers; dirges for the dead, and love-songs.

At Kalihi, a valley about two miles from the city of Honolulu is a large free school for natives which was endowed by C. R. Bishop, the American banker, from money left by his wife, the Princess Bernice Pauahi, a noble-minded and most agreeable Hawaiian lady. It was to be used for the benefit of her people.

In the centre of the numerous school buildings stands a museum where are now to be found, amongst many other curiosities, the articles displayed in the accompanying photograph. This collection had belonged to the Queen-Dowager, wife of the late King Kalakaua, and was for many years exhibited in a room of the Iolani palace in Honolulu. Most

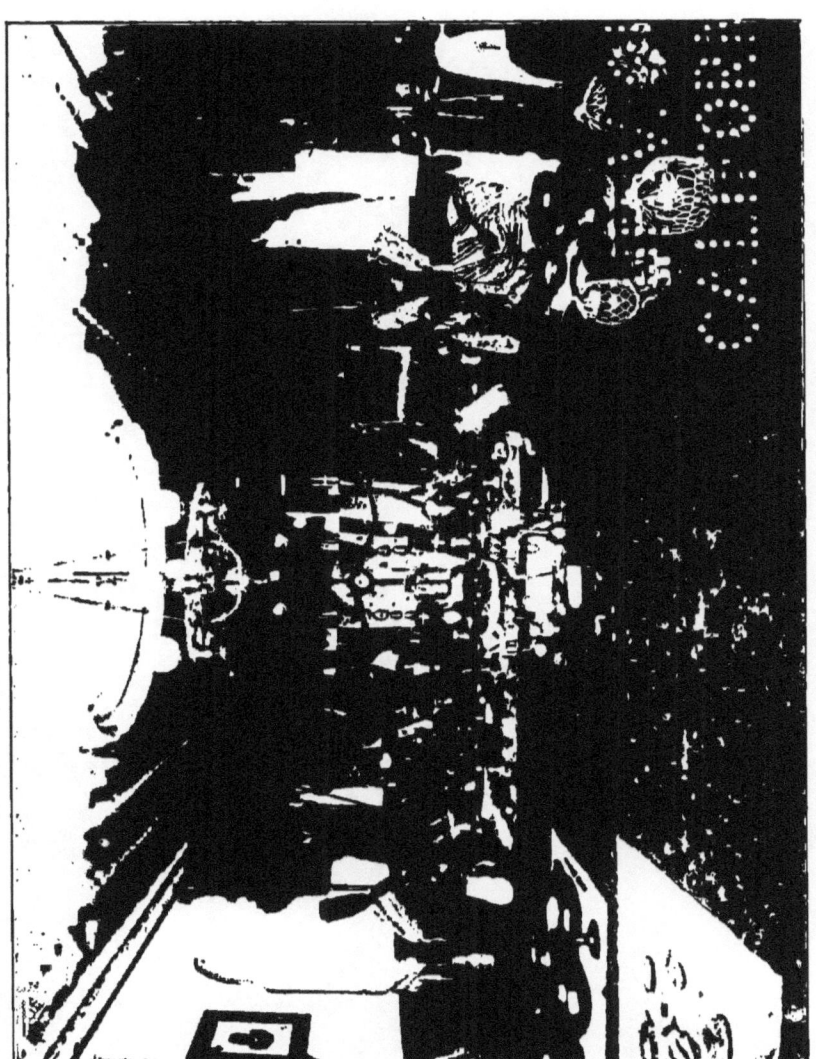

COLLECTION OF HAWAIIAN CURIOSITIES MADE BY THE DOWAGER QUEEN KAPIOLANI

noticeable in the picture are the beautiful kahilis, which stand round the room, many of them having quite a history of their own; one, of pure white, was made expressly for the funeral of the Princess Bernice Pauahi.

These kahilis are in appearance rather like a huge feather-duster, but they are formed with infinite care by the Hawaiians from the feathers of rare birds, the long handles being made of ivory or tortoise-shell.

Mrs. Judd, writing from Honolulu in 1828, telling of an excursion she made with her husband on the mountains, gives some interesting details about these feather treasures. Auwae, the chief of Wailuku, a district on the island of Maui, had invited them to visit him and on their arrival welcomed them most cordially. He had been one of the "savants" in the train of the all-conquering Kamehameha and was both an astronomer and a botanist. He placed rows of stones to show them how plants were classified and gave the native name for each.

Auwae proposed to take Dr. and Mrs. Judd to the other side of the island whence they had to set sail for Honolulu, over the mountains, instead of by sea in canoes which was the usual way of going. To give the expedition in the lady's own words. "A company of twenty-five athletic men trained to bird-catching on these beetling crags were called out, their toe and finger nails, never cut, grow like claws. Their sole business is to catch the little black birds called *oo*, each producing only two or three yellow feathers under the wings. When these are plucked the birds are set at liberty, to be caught and plundered again at some future time. Five feathers constitute a tax and are equivalent to one dollar in money. These feathers are wrought into cloaks, capes, wreaths and kahilis to bedeck royalty. The feathers, time, and labour consumed in making a cloak, now in the possession of the young king, have been estimated as amounting to hundreds of thousands of dollars. The way grew rugged and more difficult as we ascended till our heads became giddy and our feet weary, when our guides would catch us up and carry us along as though we were children. The descent on the other side of the mountains was almost perpendicular, and we swung down from branch to branch among the trees, our only security being the faithful bird-catchers who placed our feet for us and guarded each step."

In 1845 another traveller gives a description of a feather cloak he saw. "It was," he says, "made of very minute yellow feathers, two or three only being produced by a single bird, and attached with great skill to a fine net, or gauze, so as to form a brilliant and even garment, resembling somewhat delicate and malleable plates of fine gold. There were also some smaller feather capes of scarcely less beauty than the cloak." It is said that it took nine generations of kings to complete the cloak of Kamehameha I.

The large kahilis were borne as banners before and around the kings and chiefs on state occasions and especially at state funerals. The smaller were used as fly brushes and fans, and were waved day and night over the living monarchs as they sat, as well as over the dead when they lay in state surrounded by their courtiers.

In the early days they were used by watchers over the coffin that contained one of the royal family for many weeks before he was laid in the ground.

On one side of an illustration we give is shown spread on a white cloth, a small display of native sweetmeats made of coco-nut mixed with sweet potato, and also taro and kukui nuts mingled with the juice of the coco-nut. This is the dessert of a Hawaiian feast. The feast itself is a much more satisfying affair, being composed of poi, the staple native food, answering to our bread, pig, chicken, fish, and sometimes dog. The pig, chicken and dog are cooked underground, in a hole which has been previously heated with burning wood and lined with red-hot stones, on the hot stones water is poured. The meats are wrapped up in ti leaves, broad, long leaves, the earth is heaped over them and they are allowed to remain all night and until just before required, when they are produced in a far more tender state than by any other way of cooking. The fish is cooked in the same way. These substantial viands are accompanied by raw fish and sea-weed, raw "*opais*," which are very like English shrimps and prawns, dried fish and jerked beef, tinned salmon mixed with tomatoes into a kind of salad and flavoured with onions and shalots. I have seen the shrimps wriggling out of the grasp of an elegantly dressed princess as she ate them. The table-cloths are spread on the ground under shady trees and decorated with ferns and flowers, and heaps of commoner ferns

A FEAST IN NATIVE STYLE

The Origin of the Hawaiians

are spread on each side of the cloth as seats. Upon these the guests half recline as they eat—with the fingers of course—chattering fast and merrily.

To go back to our picture of curios, in the centre sits an albino. An albino appears from time to time amongst the Hawaiian race making a strange contrast to the usual black-haired, brown-skinned native. Before her are displayed various gourds, or water bottles, and calabashes, or native bowls, formed some from coco-nuts, others from handsome native woods such as the "*koa*" and the "*kou*" pronounced ko—which are capable of taking a very high polish. These are used to hold the poi, which is a paste of about the consistency of our treacle, and also as finger bowls, for after a native feast, these semi-civilised yet cleanly people stand greatly in need of a little wash. The large covered calabashes in nets, and balanced at each end of a pole, are containers of poi for sale. They are balanced over the shoulder, and carried in this way about the town.

Around the room are hung native mats woven from the long leaf of the "*lauhala*" tree and from the fibre of the coco-nut and bamboo.

Also pieces of tapa, a handsome and expensive native cloth made from beating out the bark of trees, some kinds of which when placed in windows look wondrously like stained glass.

Again we see long strings of shells, some of which are white and small, called from the name of the island where they are chiefly found, Niihau shells. Others there are, rarer and larger, of all shades of blue, purple and green. Necklaces and bracelets are also made from the kukui nut. It has the appearance of being carved as the nut is deeply fluted. Then there are seed bags and also necklets of many different sizes and colours from a rich brown to scarlet and white.

In the middle of the largest group of curiosities is a native canoe with its paddle, and on each side are poi pounders made of stone. Spears, clubs and daggers are hung in warlike profusion around the wall, reminding us that these gentle kindly Hawaiians have still running in their veins the blood of a warlike and powerful race.

CHAPTER IV

THE GODDESS OF THE GREAT VOLCANOES*

There are some interesting traditions in connection with the volcanoes on the largest island, Hawaii; and chief of all the active volcanoes in the world is that of Kilauea. Its great pit of fire is nine miles in circumference, and the main feature of its usual condition is the existence of one or more lakes of molten bubbling lava.

The natives believed formerly that these burning mountains were the homes of a terrible fiery family, who came over the sea from Tahiti, and settled in Hawaii. The names of some of these genii translated were, "The-explosion-in-the-place-of life," The Rain-of-night," Thundering-Tane," and "The Fire-thrusting-child-of-war.

These four were brothers, and two of them were crooked and humpbacked. Then came

* From my own little book afore-mentioned now out of print.

the chief goddess of Kilauea, who was called Pele; and the burning lava spray driven by the wind into what looks like threads of finely spun glass, is called Pele's hair.

After Pele comes "Fiery-eyed canoe-breaker," "Heaven-rending cloud-holder," "Heaven-dwelling cloud-holder," "Quick-glancing-eyed cloud-holder," or the cloud-holder whose eyes turn quickly and look often over her shoulders; "The Red-hot mountain-lifting clouds," "Wreath-encircled cloud-holder," and "Young cloud-holder." These were all sisters, and the whole family, as soon as they landed, made Kilauea their home. Whenever the natives mentioned their names it was with fear and trembling.

Although Kilauea was their chief abode, they had other houses, some of them on the tops of the snow-covered mountains; and when they were staying in these, on a visit, the red fire came up and lit up the snow with a rosy glow which could be seen from very far off. Often these visits were foretold by the priests at the places of sacrifice, and when they drew near the earth trembled, and there were flashes of lightning, and awful roars of thunder. They never went about doing good to anybody, only to receive offerings, or to do deeds of vengeance and anger. The people say, "Great indeed is the number of men slain by them; and four hundreds, four hundreds, four hundreds of hogs have been thrown to them." This repetition of the number four hundred means four hundred many times multiplied.

There are pleasant refreshing berries called *ohelos* growing near the great volcano; but when Mr. Ellis, the missionary, was visiting Kilauea fifty-five years ago, he gathered some and ate them, as he felt hungry and thirsty. The natives who were with him, began to cry aloud and to beg him not to do this, as they said they belonged to the goddess Pele, and might not be tasted until some had first been offered to her, and permission asked of her before they ate any themselves. Mr. Ellis told them the fruits of the earth all belonged to our God, who was glad for His people to eat them when they were hungry. But the natives said, "We are afraid some great evil will happen to us before we leave this place;" and they shook their heads and walked on silently, until they came to the edge of the great crater; then they each plucked a branch covered with berries, and threw one part of it into the burning lake of fire, saying, "Pele, here are your ohelo berries; we offer some to you, some we also eat." They told Mr. Ellis that if these beings were insulted in any way, they filled the crater with burning lava and spouted it out; or else they marched along through passages underneath the earth, to one of their other houses, and punished the people from it. If the men did not take enough up to them from the sea-shore they would rush down and kill all the fish with burning lava; fill up the shallow places with it, and destroy all their fishing grounds.

Often and often they had been attacked by other great gods, and once were nearly driven off the island by a monster called Tamapuaa, a gigantic being, half hog and half man. He came over from Oahu, and visited all the smaller islands of the Sandwich group. He also travelled, as the natives say, "to countries beyond the heavens"; that is, beyond where the heavens appear to rest on the sea. The sight of Kilauea impressed him so strongly that he asked for the hand of the goddess Pele in marriage. When, however, she saw his huge hideous shape standing on the edge of the crater she rejected his offer with great scorn and contempt, calling him "a hog and the son of a hog." As he still persisted in his advances, she rose up from the centre of the crater to drive him away, and a fierce struggle took place between them. Pele, having the weaker physical frame of the two, was driven back into her deep home down below, and Tamapuaa poured wave after wave of the sea down upon her, until the crater was almost full, and her great fires were nearly put out. Pele, in despair, called her sisters together and took counsel. They drank up all the waters between them. She rose again, accompanied by them, and this time they managed to drive the monster down into the sea, following him with thunder, lightning, and immense stones.

In old times the island of Hawaii had its own kings. The last of these, named Keona, displeased Pele very much; some say he did not offer enough hogs and fish to the goddess, others that he ate her ohelo berries and pulled up the sacred grass that surrounded her dwelling. However that may have been, she became exceedingly angry with him, and determined to help his enemy Kamehameha, the ancestor of the last race of kings. She shook the earth terribly, and sent up a column of dense black smoke followed by bright red flames. Streams of lava spouted up and ran down over the sides of the crater, and huge rocks were shot up into the air. Showers of smaller stones that flew much faster came closely over the rocks, and when they touched these the rocks burst with a sound like thunder and vivid flashes of lightning lit up the country all round. Many of Keona's people were killed by the falling pieces of rock, and many others smothered and buried beneath the ashes and lava. Keona was a strong and brave man; he continued his march and fought with courage, until he was completely overpowered by his rival. This story of the fight for supremacy between the two chief rulers, and of the terrible eruption which hindered and destroyed Keona's army, is perfectly true, and the Hawaiians believed thoroughly in Pele's part in the tragedy.

The whole history of Hawaii has been wrapt in wonder and mystery, and we cannot be surprised that the natives should tell marvellous stories of its origin. One tradition they have is that an immense bird laid an egg on the water, which burst and produced the island, and that soon afterwards a man, a woman, a

The Goddess of the Great Volcanoes

hog, a dog, and a pair of fowls came in a canoe from Tahiti, and settled upon it.

One more story about Pele. A chief of Hawaii was amusing himself, with one of his companions, in sliding down the steep side of a hill on a narrow wooden sledge. Crowds of people gathered at the foot of the hill to watch the sport, and musicians and dancing girls and youths were there also. The race between Kahavari and his favourite began, whilst the drums and songs and dances formed a gay accompaniment. Pele was disturbed in her high mountain home by the festive sounds, so she came down to see the fun. In the shape of an ordinary woman, she stood on the top of a hill and challenged the chief to slide with her. He accepted the challenge, and away they started together. Powerful and clever as Pele was she did not know how to balance herself properly on a narrow sledge, so she was beaten, and the people shouted Kahavari's praises as he walked back up the hillside. Pele did not want to feel herself quite beaten, so, before they started again, she asked him to lend her his sledge. Never dreaming that she was a goddess, as she looked just like any other woman, he replied :

"No! Are you my wife that you should have my sledge?"

Then he set it right, jumped upon it, running a few yards first so as to take a spring, and shot off swiftly down the hill.

Pele was furious; she stamped on the ground, and created an earthquake which rent the hill in sunder. Then she cried aloud, and fire and lava arose, which followed her down the hill, so that when Kahavari reached the bottom he saw Pele, with thunder and lightning, earthquake and streams of burning lava, flying down after him. He took up his broad spear, which he had stuck in the ground before beginning the race, and fled for his life, his friend with him. The musicians, the dancers, and crowds of merrymakers were buried altogether beneath the fiery streams, which, carrying in front of them the insulted and angry goddess, still pursued Kahavari and his companion. The two ran on until they came to a little hill, where Kahavari threw off his cloak of woven leaves. Then he went down towards his house on the seashore. The first creature he met there was his favourite hog. He saluted it by touching noses, and ran on to the house of his mother, with whom he also touched noses, saying:

The Goddess of the Great Volcanoes

"Compassion great to you! Close here, perhaps, is your death; Pele comes devouring!"

Leaving her, he next met his wife, whom he also saluted. The burning torrent was quickly drawing near them, and she said:

"Stay with me here and let us die together."

"No; I go, I go," he answered.

Next he saluted his two boys, and said, "I grieve for you two."

The fiery stream came on, and he ran till he was stopped by a deep chasm.

Across this he laid his spear, over which he walked safely. His friend was still following closely behind and he cried for help, Kahavari held the spear towards him so that he also was able to cross in safety.

And now Pele came faster than ever; still Kahavari was ahead of her. Next he met his sister, but he had only time to cry out, "Alas! for you," as he ran on to the seashore. His younger brother had just landed from his fishing canoe, and had run up to his house to try and get his family into some place of safety, when Kahavari arrived.

The two friends leaped into the poor brother's canoe, and with Kahavari's broad spear paddled out to sea. When Pele saw they had escaped she ran to the shore and hurled huge stones and pieces of rock after the canoe, which, however, escaped injury. When they had paddled out some way from the shore, an east wind sprang up. Fixing the broad spear upright in the canoe, Kahavari made it serve both as mast and sail, so that they soon reached the Island of Maui, where they rested one night, and then went on to Lanai. The next day they landed on Molokai, and from that island they passed to Oahu, where the two men settled.

"Kapiolani"—whom Tennyson has commemorated in verse—writes a native historian, "was one of the noblest characters of her time. Though at one time intemperate and dissolute, Kapiolani became an example to her countrywomen of virtue and refinement, and excelled them all in the readiness with which she adopted civilised habits and sentiments. In December, 1824, she determined to break the spell of the belief in Pele, the dread goddess of the volcano. In spite of the strenuous opposition of her friends, and even of her husband, she made a journey of about one hundred and fifty miles, mostly on foot, from Kealakekua to Hilo, visiting the great crater of Kilauea on her way, in order to defy the wrath of Pele, and to prove that no such being existed. On approaching the volcano, she met the priestess of Pele, who warned her not to go near the crater, and predicted her death if she violated the tabus of the goddess. 'Who are you?' demanded Kapiolani. 'One in whom the goddess dwells,' she replied. Kapiolani quoted passages from the Scriptures, setting forth the character and power of the true God, until the priestess was silenced, and confessed that the akua, or deity, had left her. Kapiolani then went forward to the crater where in full view of the grand and terrific action of the inner crater, she ate the berries consecrated to Pele, and threw stones into the burning lake, saying, 'Jehovah is my God. He kindleth these fires. I fear not Pele. If I perish by her anger, then you may fear Pele; but if I trust in Jehovah, and He preserves me when breaking her tabus, then you must fear and serve Him alone.' They then united in singing a hymn of praise to the true God, and knelt in adoration to the Creator and Governor of the universe." This has been well called "one of the greatest acts of moral courage ever performed." Kapiolani told a lady to whom I am indebted later, Mrs. Judd, a story of her childhood, which showed how independent a character she had always been. Under the old *régime*, bananas and certain kinds of fish were forbidden to women. One day she, with another girl of her own age and rank, resolved to taste the forbidden fruit. They held it as well hidden in the hand as they could, and ran into the sea to eat it whilst bathing. A keen-eyed priest saw them in the act and they were tried, and condemned to the penalty of breaking this tabu—that of poverty, loss of rank, and to remain unmarried, unless suitable expiation could be made. This the priest suggested, should be the sacrifice of a little boy, a favourite page of Kapiolani's.* The poor child was seized and carried to the sacred enclosure. When Kapiolani asked what had become of him the old priest told her he had been strangled on the altar. She hid her face and wept as she repeated the story, adding, " Why did not Christians come sooner and teach us better things."

Some years after her brave act of defiance Kapiolani went on a visit to the doctor's, and had a cancer removed from her breast. When

* Professor Alexander says it was a favourite tutor who was made a victim of Kapiolani's temerity. This is, however, immaterial.

the surgeons entered to perform the operation she was excited and nervous and asked for a few moments that she might pray alone. Soon she returned, and with a calm dignity sat down to submit to the knife. Now, writes Mrs. Judd in her diary, " her heart is too full of gratitude for the recovery of her health, she cannot be quiet a moment and wants to enlist all hearts in a song of praise." Unfortunately a walk in the hot sun brought on erysipelas, and this noble chiefess died very suddenly.

CHAPTER V

THE FIRST KINGS OF UNITED HAWAII

THE first two-and-a-half centuries after the eventful and disturbing times of the Southern navigators' visits were peaceful and prosperous, and the chiefs are said to have been wise rulers on the whole, during whose lives many useful works were completed; but about the end of the thirteenth century an ambitious high chief of the island of Hawaii set himself to conquer all the other kings and chiefs. He was, however, defeated in the island of Kauai, always the home of a sturdy race. Wars now became frequent, and the natives of a more sanguinary turn.

About the beginning of the sixteenth century a foreign vessel was wrecked off Hawaii; only the captain and his sister landed. They were welcomed by the people, and ended by marrying among them and becoming the progenitors of

The First Kings of United Hawaii 103

some of the chiefs best known in later history. These are supposed to have been Spaniards, the survivors of two lost vessels that had been fitted out by Cortez the conqueror of Mexico. In 1555 these islands were also visited, it is said, by the Spanish navigator Juan Gaetano. Proof of this is contained in Spanish archives.

During one of the inter-island wars of this period, on a stormy November night in the year 1736, the first of the Kamehamehas was born, the ruler who was to subdue the whole group, uniting them into one kingdom. As a young prince he distinguished himself, being both brave and accomplished in all national sports and games. He was just over forty years of age when Captain Cook made his first visit to the islands.

To the death of our famous navigator I allude elsewhere. His fate had such an effect on the outside world that no vessel touched at the group for more than seven years.

Kamehameha was ever a bold and fearless character. On that account his uncle, the then King of Hawaii, advised him at one time to retire from the court to his own estates at Kohala. There he dwelt for two years, in peaceful and useful activity. A tunnel which he constructed in order to carry water through a ridge in the mountains is still shown, besides a canoe landing-place that he had made, and a fishpond, with other works. He improved his district much during that quiet time at Kohala. But when dissensions among the high chiefs broke out, Kamehameha could not remain neutral. Then came what is termed "the bitter war" in which his forces were routed; and again he returned to his peaceful life at Kohala. About the year 1785 he married Kaahumauu, later a notable figure in Hawaiian history.

Space will not allow me to tell of Kamehameha's wars and many deeds of prowess, until he had made himself by conquest of the other kings and high chiefs, king of the entire group of islands. A prominent character—one who helped him greatly—was John Young, an English sailor, boatswain, who was detained from an American fur-trading vessel, which had put in at the islands. Valuable land was bestowed on him, and he was made a chief, one of the royal family being given to him later as wife. Another white man named Davis, who afterwards met his death through his loyalty to the King of Kauai, then under

Kamehameha's protection, was also detained with Young.

There was a great eruption of lava from one of the volcanoes during this period, and after hundreds of hogs had been thrown in to appease the anger in Pele, Kamehameha cut off part of his hair which was held sacred, and threw it into the flowing lava. It ceased to flow a day or two later, a circumstance which was considered to be of the highest significance by the whole of the people.

Honolulu in 1809 consisted of a village of a few hundred huts. The king's house was built close to the shore, shaded by coco-palms, and surrounded by a palisade. The British colours were displayed there, and a battery of sixteen carriage guns that belonged to his ship were ranged about it.

Another foreigner, besides John Young and Isaac Davis, did good service here between 1791 and 1837. This was Don Francisco de Paula Marin from Andalusia. He acted as interpreter to the king; but also taught many useful industries, growing oranges, figs, grapes, pine-apples, &c. He made their first butter, too, and wine, and he salted beef. So much sandalwood was sold at this time that the natives on

Hawaii brought about a famine by neglecting agriculture to cut this wood. The king then went to Hawaii and set his attendants to till the ground, himself working with them. He forbade the cutting of the young sandal-wood trees, and another humane act was to order the birdcatchers to spare the birds from which they plucked the prized yellow feathers, from under the wing, for the royal cloaks. They had been wont to strangle the birds, which they caught by smearing the branches with sticky gum, and baiting them with the favourite flowers of the birds. Professor Alexander tells us that " these birds were honey suckers, living on the nectar of the ohia, the banana and the large lobelias. The yellow feathers were taken from two species of birds, the oo (*Acrulocercus nobilis*), which has one little tuft of yellow feathers under each wing, and the still rarer mamo, *Drepanis pacifica*, which has larger golden yellow feathers on its back. The latter species is nearly extinct. The scarlet feathers were obtained from the *iiwi*, *Vestiaria coccinea*, a song bird with gorgeous scarlet coat and black wings, and from the *Fringilla coccinea*.

In 1809 the Russian governor of Alaska had an idea of forming a colony in the Hawaiian islands, and a Scotch captain, Archibald Campbell, visited them on his ship *Neva*. In 1815, the *Myrtle*, a Russian ship was sent from Alaska, and she anchored at Honolulu. The Russians landed, built a block-house, mounted a few guns, and hoisted their nation's flag. Kamehameha sent a large force of chiefs and warriors to watch the aggressors, and, if necessary, to resist with arms. But the night after they arrived in Honolulu the *Myrtle* and a Russian brig, which had put in for repairs, both sailed for the island of Kauai and they remained some time at Hanalei, threw up a breast-work, and mounted a few cannon there. A Dr. Scheffer had a year previously been sent to Kauai by M. Baranoff, the Governor of Alaska; and this man had persuaded the King of Kauai, who, though he had been subdued by the King of Hawaii still held his own islands in fief, to give him the beautiful and fertile valley of Hanalei. He had superintended the building of a fort for the ex-king. Over it the Russian colours now floated.

Kamehameha sent a messenger with orders to expel these Russians, and Dr. Scheffer at once betook himself, with his property, to Honolulu on the Russian brig. The ship

Myrtle was also requested to leave, but she proved not seaworthy; she had to put back, and sank in the harbour. Soon after a Russian war sloop touched at the islands, and made inquiries. Captain Kotzebue called a year later, and at first caused great anxiety, until he assured the king that he did not come officially.

M. Choris, an artist who accompanied Kotzebue in his expedition—one of discovery—painted the only portrait there is of the great Kamehameha. It is on one of the early postage stamps, and will be familiar to all collectors. When the king understood Kotzebue's mission, he treated him most generously; his ship, the *Rurick*, was towed into harbour by eight double canoes, and every assistance was given to the expedition. On his part he gave two eight pounder mortars, with a supply of shells, powder, etc.

Our own Captain Vancouver's mission was chiefly one of peace, "the object he had most at heart," says Professor Alexander, "was to bring about a lasting peace between Hawaii and the Leeward Islands." So he always refused to part with any firearms or ammunition to the king or any of the high chiefs; telling them, right loyally, that "his ship and all it contained belonged to King George, who had tabued all fire-arms and ammunition."

It seems to me a matter of great interest to dwell on the way in which the nations acted in regard to these beautiful islands, and their gracious, hospitable people. "Am I my brother's keeper?" was about the earliest problem presented in that book by which a Christian government professes to rule its conduct to the outside world. Unfortunately, we sent at one time our vilest subjects "for their country's good," away to leaven other people, and one of the results was that some Botany Bay convicts introduced the art of distilling ardent spirits into these islands at the end of the eighteenth century. A William Stevenson, from New South Wales, was the first to practise it; under his direction the root of the *Ki* plant, *Cordyline terminalis*, was baked first for some days in the ground—native fashion—which made it very sweet. Then it was bruised in a canoe with water to ferment it, and in five or six days it was ready for the still, which was rudely formed of iron pots, got from ships, with a gun-barrel for a tube, to conduct the vapour. The result was a nearly pure alcohol. Soon nearly every chief had his separate still.

The demoralising effect was incalculable. Rum was then also imported largely. At first, Kamehameha gave way to excesses, but John Young, then made Governor of Hawaii, happily convinced him of the evil. By degrees he accustomed himself to occasional small quantities and at last he abstained entirely. Before he died, he called a great assembly of all the chief men on Hawaii, when he ordered all the stills to be destroyed and forbade any further manufacture of intoxicating liquor. Well, indeed, would it have been if his chiefs could have adhered to the same resolution. But, alas, there are "Ghosts!" as Ibsen has it; his own son and successor, Kamehameha II., drank to excess, and many of the chiefs followed his bad example.

A lawless set of Spanish pirates followed the Russians, but these were under the command of an Englishman named Turner. The crew spent most of their time in revelry on shore, and they sold their ship to the king. It turned out that they had run away with a sloop of war, the *Santa Rosa*, which belonged to La Plata; they had pillaged a town on the coast of Chili and robbed the churches of gold and silver, crucifixes, candelabra, sacrament cups, &c., and re-christened the sloop as the *Victory*.

A Spanish man-of-war arrived a few months afterwards, and informed Kamehameha of their true character. At once he sent out emissaries who succeeded in securing most of the buccaneers and they were delivered up to justice. The church property was most of it recovered and given up to the captain of the *Argentina*, and the first officer of the pirates, who had fled to Kauai, was executed on the beach at Waimea.

Kamehameha was eighty-two years old when he died in 1819. A noble character was his, in the main. He had united the ever-warring islands under one head, and truly prepared the way for civilisation and that Christian teaching which the American mission brought five years later.

The usual human sacrifices were not made, it is believed at his death. It is said that during his last illness he expressed a desire to that effect. His very words are said to have been: "The men are sacred to the king," meaning his successor. He enjoined his son to live in the faith of his ancestors, and to respect the tabu.

Immediately after his death, however, as was the national custom, all restraints were taken away for a time. Liholiho, Kamehameha II., violated the tabu, licence prevailed, and the state of the country was frightful.

And this evil condition of things lasted for some years. An aged lady, Mrs. Thurston, who lived near us in Nuuanu Valley, with whom I much enjoyed talking about these early days, told me that when she arrived with the first missionaries, the ship lay outside, until the heads of the party assured themselves it was wise to land with their wives. Five days these had to remain on board, in the harbour, because the whole town of Honolulu lay drunk and naked outside the doors of their huts.

Knowing his son's unfitness to govern, the late king had appointed his favourite queen to be *Kuhina nui*, that is Regent, his *Kahu*, or guardian she already was. But now she could exercise equal authority with the young king.

On the very morning of the death of her husband, six chiefs proposed to her that the tabu should be renounced. The visits of so many foreigners, and the absence, with them, of like restraints, had had great influence over the minds of the Hawaiians. Ten days later, when the time of retirement was over, Kaahumanu, the Regent, proposed at their first grand public appearance that the tabu should be disregarded for the future. The king did not at first consent, as he remembered his father's dying injunctions. That evening the queen-mother sent for a younger son to break the tabu by eating with her. Poor weak young king, he yielded soon, and on Kaahumanu expressing her desire that idolatry should be abolished, he embarked with his retinue in several canoes, spent two whole days in a drunken debauch and broke the tabu again and again. A great royal feast, of both sexes together, was then held; and when the common people, who looked on in superstitious fear, saw that no harm came of it, they shouted: "The tabus are at an end and the gods are a lie." The high priest next set fire to the idols, messengers proclaimed the abolition of the tabu all over the islands and general licence prevailed.

One brave and popular young chief, however, was indignant. He retired from his fellows, and some of the best of the priests gathered round him and offered to get the people to rally round him and to make him their king. They reiterated an ancient Hawaiian proverb which is curiously like a Bible text: "A religious chief shall possess the kingdom, but irreligious chiefs shall always be poor."

A number of chiefs rallied round the brave Kekuaokalani, and a chief was killed; but the Queen-Regent, Kaahumanu, who had been indulging in debauched revelry with her friends, suddenly pulled herself together and sent to try and propitiate the insurgents. The late king had recently bought a great number of muskets and much ammunition, from an American trader, and these gained the day for Kaahumanu and her followers. Ellis gives a pathetic account of what was the end of the noble-minded young chief. He relates how when he could resist no longer, being unable to stand from loss of blood, "he sat on a fragment of lava and twice loaded and fired his musket at the advancing foe. He now received a ball in the left breast, and, covering his face with his feather cloak, expired in the midst of his men.

"His wife, Manono, during the whole of the battle had fought by his side with steady and dauntless courage. A few moments after her husband's death she called out for quarter, but

The First Kings of United Hawaii

the words had hardly left her lips before she received a bullet in her left temple; fell upon the lifeless body of her husband and expired." Their followers lost courage and were soon dispersed.

The people then turned against their idols in contempt, and slew the chief adviser of the brave insurgent, a priest. Images and sacred enclosures were burned, and as Kaahumanu, a little later, collected all that remained hidden away, Hawaii was left without a religion, and without the tabu.

How often have I been told from English and Americans that missionaries have harmed the simple Polynesians by making them do away with the salutary and wise tabus. Yet here was a nation that had cast them away before a missionary showed himself in their midst. True, they had been influenced for evil by foreigners, but these were Botany Bay convicts, beech-combers, and wanderers from all nations, who sought, with a few noble exceptions, only their own interests.

The rejection of their old religion and the abolition of the tabu system happened in 1819, and curiously enough the first mission party from America sailed in the very same month that the last burning of idols occurred, from Boston, for the voyage round Cape Horn to Honolulu.

In spite of these great changes many superstitions survived, and sorcery still held sway over the minds of the people.

"You will probably none of you live to witness the downfall of idolatry," were among the last words said to the mission party as they embarked. Five months later, when anchored in Kailua Bay, Hopu, one of their company and their interpreter—a young Hawaiian who had been carried away on a whaler, and educated in New England—landed first, and brought back to them from the shore the tidings, "Liholiho is king; the tabus are abolished; the idols are burned; the temples are destroyed. There has been war but now there is peace." The king wearing a malo—or loin cloth—a green silk mantle over the right shoulder, a string of beads round his neck, and a wreath of yellow feathers on his head, soon came on board to dine with them. John Young used all his influence in their favour, telling the chiefs that these were of the same religion as those English teachers whom the good Captain Vancouver had promised to send them. The mission party consisted of two clergymen and their wives, and five laymen and their wives.

"The first pupils of the missionaries," writes Alexander, "were the chiefs and their favourite attendants, and the wives and children (half castes) of foreigners. At first their teaching was entirely in English, but by degrees they devoted their time and energies more and more to the task of mastering the Hawaiian language, and of reducing it to writing until they made it their chief medium of instruction."

Of the second Kamehameha there is little to tell. He forsook the friends and advisers of his father, and chose his favourites and guides from a low set of adventurous white men. Soon he was involved in debt. Sandal-wood, much of it too young, was sold in large quantities, but to little purpose.

When, in 1823, there was an annual feast in commemoration of his accession, his wives, and his brother, and sister were borne in state. The queen-mother was seated in a whaleboat, borne on the shoulders of seventy men, whose outer ranks wore scarlet and yellow feather cloaks and helmets. The queen in scarlet silk and coronet of feathers, sat under a huge umbrella of scarlet, supported by a chief in a scarlet malo and feather helmet. Kahilis, "the plumed staffs of state," twenty feet high, waved aloft. One of the queens wore seventy-two yards of orange and scarlet kerseymere. Several hundreds of dancing girls encircled the highest chiefs, singing their praises as they proceeded.

But alas! it was the play of *Hamlet* minus Hamlet, for the king with his special attendants was riding, intoxicated and nearly naked. Their horses had no saddles, and fifty or sixty low and dirty natives on foot ran after them.

The head queen, his mother, had a Tahitian Christian chaplain, and taking him, as well as two of the American mission party with her, she now moved to Lahaina on Maui, founding the mission there. Soon after this she died, after being baptized by Mr. Ellis, who was just then exploring the island of Hawaii, assisted by three of the American party. The Rev. W. Ellis had arrived from Tahiti with Captain Kent, who brought a schooner of seventy tons, the *Prince Regent*, with six guns, which had been built, in New South Wales, by the British Government, in fulfilment of a promise made by Vancouver to Kamehameha I. Two of

The First Kings of United Hawaii

the London Society's missionaries and two Tahitian Christian teachers were also on board. The whole party were on their way to the Marquesas and they stayed in Honolulu four months, whilst Captain Kent, in his brig, went on to Fanning's Island for "bêche de mer."

So heartily were these welcomed by the chiefs and the mission that they gave up the plan of settling in the Marquesas, and devoted themselves to Hawaii. The language of the Hawaiians and the Tahitians is so nearly alike, that Mr. Ellis could preach well to the former in two months' time.

It was about this time that the king decided to visit England and the United States. He had a desire to secure protection for his country against Russia, whose men-of-war, visiting his country, had made him uneasy. He wanted Mr. Ellis to go with him, but Captain Starbuck, the American captain of the English whale-ship, on which the king and queen with their suite sailed, absolutely refused to take him. This made the people uneasy, and they left them full of forebodings of evil. The death, in London, of Liholiho and his queen, Kamamalu, confirmed these fears. The queen died first, of measles, and this affected the king so much that he sickened and only survived her a few days.

Boki, a high chief, and his wife Liliha, of whom I shall tell more presently, and three others had accompanied them to England, and they had been most kindly received. King George IV. had welcomed them at Windsor where he advised them to profit by the teachings of their missionaries and promised them his protection against all foreign aggression.

Lord Byron, a cousin of the poet, was ordered to convey the remains of the ill-fated pair, with their attendants, back to Hawaii, in the forty-six gun frigate, the *Blonde*. The scene on the arrival in Honolulu was most affecting.

A gold watch was given, as a present from the British Government, to Kalanimoku, the Prime Minister, who had been baptized William Pitt, a silver teapot to the Queen Regent, Kaahumanu, and a rich suit of uniform with hat and sword to the little prince, who was soon proclaimed as Kamehameha III. The *Blonde* sailed for Hilo next day with the Queen Regent and her suite on board. Lord Byron, with the scientists in his company, visited the volcano, occupying the hut of Kapiolani, who had, the year previously, defied the goddess Pele there. He was a man who won the love and respect of all alike.

"If," says Professor Alexander, "he had left there a suitable representative of his government, imbued with his own humane and enlightened views, the subsequent history of the islands would have been very different."

Lord Byron persuaded the chiefs to endeavour to suppress the vices which were their ruin, and to promote education. But their seaports being now frequently visited by a lawless set of unscrupulous foreigners, who were bent only on their own pleasure and profit, drunkenness and prostitution prevailed, and to the disgrace of England, the British Consul of the time, Mr. Charlton, denied the right of the native chiefs to make laws without the approval of the British Government. When laws were at last framed, the crew of the first ship, the *Daniel* from London—God save the mark—that arrived in the port of Lahaina after this, finding that changes had occurred since their last visit, and foiled in their evil propensities, "entered the house of Mr. Richards, one of the American mission party, and threatened him and his wife with death if they did not procure the repeal of the obnoxious law. Their calm and heroic demeanour seems to have saved their lives." Four days later, however, a larger company landed, under a black flag, and armed with knives and pistols, and forced an entrance into the yard. Mr. Richards had been placed over the Lahaina mission by the queen-mother, and the natives being loyal to their teachers, now interfered and saved them. The chief, Hoapili, ever a loyal spirit, placed a strong armed guard over the station, until the *Daniel* left Lahaina.

Then followed the outrage of the *Dolphin*, an armed schooner of the United States, with Lieutenant John Percival in charge. An American ship had been wrecked at Lania and he went from Honolulu to save its cargo. On his return to the capital he called on the queen regent and demanded the repeal of the law against vice, with the infamous plea that the condition of his crew required it. Not obtaining what he wished, his men attacked the houses of the native Prime Minister, who was ill, and also the mission premises, doing much damage; Mr. Bingham only escaped with his life.

"In the evening Lieutenant Percival waited

on the chiefs, and again insisted on the repeal of the law. At length Governor Boki, the high chief, and Maniua, captain of the fort, intimidated by his threats, permitted its violation; at which it is said, 'a shout of triumph rang through the shipping.' The *Dolphin* remained in port two months longer, and the pernicious influence exerted by the crew during that time cannot be described."

Such was the accursed influence of the lawless white man!

On Lieutenant Percival's return to the States a court met to inquire into his conduct.

The same year the crews of several whale ships landed at Lahaina, on Maui, again threatening the lives of the mission family. Happily, these were absent in Hawaii, and a native guard kept their premises. The sailors rioted and broke open and plundered the native houses. The native women had fled to the mountains with a chiefess, who was acting as governor in Hoapili's absence, and they stayed there till the ships left.

Then some shipowners sent a memorial to the United States President complaining of the mutiny and desertion of their crews, stating that the "Sandwich Islands would become a nest of pirates and murderers." About a hundred whale ships visited the islands yearly. Captain Jones was sent in the *Peacock*, a war sloop, to attend to the matter, and "to secure certain debts due to American citizens by the native Government!" He stayed nearly three months, trying in the first place to rid the islands of the runaway sailors. No list of the audacious claims of the American traders on the young king and chiefs was ever published; yet, though Captain Jones reduced these, he made out the great sum of $500,000, and in order to pay this, every able-bodied male was forced to deliver half a pucil of sandal-wood or to pay four Spanish dollars within nine months time, and every woman who was of age had to give a mat 12 feet by 6 feet, or pay one dollar. The population was then—1827—estimated at 140,000.

A great council was convoked by the Queen-Regent, at which Mr. Charlton, the British Consul, declared that the islanders were subjects of Great Britain, and he denied their right to make foreign treaties; but Captain Jones replied that the fact of Charlton's commission as Consul recognised the independence of the islands. After this, a commercial treaty —the first made between Hawaii and a foreign power—was made with the United States.

The Chief Boki, on his return from England, had been made Governor of Oahu, and he had charge of the young king, by authority of Kaahumanu, the Queen-Regent. In a few years he and his wife began to drink, and ran into debt. Evil-minded foreigners persuaded him to act against the Queen-Regent and to lead the young king into bad ways. The Prime Minister—one whom his people called "the iron cable of Hawaii"—died also about this time, and the good cause lost ground again. A third outrage occurred at Lahaina, where an English whaler in command of an American had got several native women on board, and refused to obey Hoapili's order that they should be landed. The captain only ridiculed all representations, so Hoapili detained him on shore, seizing his boat. On the man's promise to return the women he was released, but meanwhile the crew had opened fire on the village with a nine-pound gun. Next morning Captain Clarke sailed for Honolulu, carrying away the women with him. By order of the Queen-Regent, heavy guns were now mounted at

Lahaina and the native guard was strengthened. A few days later "the first written laws were published against murder, theft, adultery, rum-selling, and gambling," and the outrages at Lahaina ceased. Before this the only written law was the Decalogue, which the Queen-Regent said "could not be improved on." Later, armed native bands paraded the streets, clearing the haunts of dissipation.

During the closing years of Kaahumanu's regency the first Roman Catholic missionaries began their work in the islands. Three priests of the order of the Congregation of the Sacred Hearts of Jesus and Mary were set apart for their mission. Their first mass was celebrated in Honolulu in a small chapel in 1828. Boki and Mr. Charlton favoured them, for purposes of their own, and a small congregation soon gathered about them; but in 1829 Governor Boki, by order of the Queen-Regent, published a decree forbidding the natives to attend the Catholic worship, and a persecution of the Roman Catholics began. The natives had to give up their crucifixes, and were threatened with punishment if they used these in their devotions. A native woman, who had been baptized in California and was in the Queen-

Regent's train, was treated harshly, and would have been sent to the little island of Kahoolawe, which was then used as a place of banishment, but for the intervention of Mr. Richards of the American Protestant Mission. So she was sent only to Honolulu. Other Catholics were punished by hard labour—building walls or braiding mats. Some offenders were even put in irons by Kaahumanu because they refused to obey where their religion was concerned.

Kaahumanu's words to the priests when they first landed had been as follows :

"We do not want you. We have put away our idols and abandoned our old system of religious forms and penances. We have received the word of God by the hand of teachers whom we love, and with whom we are satisfied. Our kingdom is a little one. We do not wish the minds of our subjects distracted by any other sect. Go away and teach destitute countries which have not received the Bible."

A council of high-chiefs was finally held, and the priests were ordered to leave the kingdom within three months. These chiefs, indeed, fitted out a vessel of their own—a brig—at great cost, and the strangers were landed at San Pedro, in California, where the Franciscan fathers welcomed them cordially. The lay brothers had been permitted to remain, and they kept their faith alive amongst the natives who had joined them, until a successful Roman Catholic Mission was again established in 1840. It has done good educational work amongst the Portuguese as well as the natives.

When Mr. Bingham, of the Protestant Mission, remonstrated with Kaahumanu for sending some Catholic converts to work on the stone walls, she pleaded that image-worship had been put down, and was a political offence, because two of their international wars had arisen solely out of religious differences. There was reason in this. At the present time all religious parties are equal, but one cannot wonder at the feeling in those early days.

CHAPTER VI

A PRACTICAL MISSION

THE burdens that were laid on the early American missionaries and their wives, and cheerfully borne by them, would astonish some who prejudice the minds of the public against foreign missions. When the party to which Dr. and Mrs. Judd belonged arrived, the Queen-Regent told them that one of the ladies must belong exclusively to her—live with her, teach her, make her gowns and instruct her women so that she could live as the foreigners did. And poor Mrs. Bingham, in the midst of her arduous teaching, was ordered to make with her own hands a dozen shirts for the king, and next, a whole suit of broadcloth. They were willing to do all if only they might win these people; so one of the ladies took to pieces a coat of her husband's, from which she carefully cut one for his Majesty, "making allowance for the larger mass of humanity that was to go in it."

Dr. and Mrs. Judd began housekeeping in "two little rooms and a chamber," under the same roof as another family of the mission. The boards were so badly joined that fearful clouds of dust were blown in by the trade-winds. A large trunk was made into a larder by setting it on stilts which stood in pans of tar water to keep out the cockroaches and white ants. Sometimes there was little in it that they could eat, and the tenderly nurtured woman of only twenty-four years says, "What if I did think of the nice little delicacies my friends in America would offer one if they could; was it wicked? Were we like the naughty Israelites, longing for the flesh-pots of Egypt? We wiped away our tears as quickly as we could."

The "we" referred to another lady who was with the doctor's wife whilst her husband was away exploring. She had been sitting up all night with a sick child, and was weary and overwrought. Their meal was salt beef that had been spoilt by a long voyage round Cape Horn, and watery sweet potatoes. Then the doctor's wife remembered that she had actually the, to her then, large sum of four shillings, that had been in her purse ever since she left Boston. She sent a native to the market, and he returned with a pound and a half of fresh beef for fifty cents. But she adds, "I know it is against the rule and would be thought a precedent; we will say nothing about it."

It was in 1828 that Dr. and Mrs. Judd landed in Honolulu, he being a physician coming under the auspices of the American Board.

Mrs. Judd devoted herself to work amongst the natives; she and the doctor were received with great favour by the Queen-Regent, Kaahumanu, who was very thankful to avail herself of the services of a skilful medical man. Mrs. Judd's diary is most fascinating reading; from it I shall give some extracts. There is so truly human a touch in the descriptions. She was an accomplished and capable woman, exactly fitted for the civilising work to which she was specially called. She and the Queen-Regent were in pleasant touch from the day she landed, when Kaahumanu sent a "yellow one-horse waggon drawn by natives and two blue hand-carts" down to the gate of the fort, where the governor, a gentlemanlike native, had received the party very graciously. They stopped at the door of the queen's house and found her to be a "tall, stately and dignified" woman, sometimes arrogant in manner, but with "a face beaming with love" whenever she spoke to her teachers. Her dress was of striped blue and pink satin, over which she wore a white muslin shawl and a Leghorn bonnet. The crowd of natives following the procession which Kaahumanu politely headed to the mission house, was a motley one in its dress, and utter undress. One man bore himself proudly carrying an umbrella, and wearing only a pair of shoes. "They laughed and jabbered, ran on in advance, and turned back to peer in our faces. I laughed and cried too, and hid my face for very shame." Even the conventional Polynesian salute is rendered prettily by Mrs. Judd. "She took us by the hand and kissed in the Hawaiian style, by placing her nose against our cheeks and giving a sniff, *as one would inhale the fragrance of flowers.*"

Her private carriage was a light hand-cart, painted turquoise-blue, spread with fine mats and beautiful velvet and damask cushions, and "her immense stateliness" was drawn by six stout men in pairs. But she rode backwards, with her feet hanging down behind the cart!

Kaahumanu had become strangely changed under the new teaching. She used to be pleasure-loving to the length of depravity, haughty, cruel and unscrupulous to gain her own ends. She was superior in intellect to the rest of the chiefs, and although she destroyed the idols, whom at heart she had always despised, she had treated the mission teachers at first with contempt, until the arts of reading and writing appealed to her high intelligence. She got interested in these, however, and was completely converted to the doctrines of the new comers. After a severe illness, during which they nursed her tenderly, they won her completely. These Americans were very wise; they taught the people the various trades and some of the arts of civilisation. Theirs was not merely book-learning and precepts. So great a change was wrought in the Queen-Regent that her people, who benefited by her change of creed and of heart, now styled her "the new Kaahumanu."

She had an adopted daughter who is called "little Ruth" in Mrs. Judd's diary. Those who remember her huge proportions, as I do, when in the islands, will smile at the idea of "little Ruth." She was a fine creature though, every way.

Then Mrs. Judd tells of "a furore for the marriage service." The Hawaiians had, in the old days, no ceremony whatever in connection with matrimony. A native who possessed a blue cloth coat with bright buttons, now rented this out to the bridegrooms. The dress of the brides was often funny enough. A ragged nightcap, "abstracted perhaps from some one's washing, or the head bandaged with a white handkerchief, tied on the top in an immense fancy knot, over which was thrown a green veil which pulled down the knot on to the nose, nearly blinding the wearer." The usual fee to the clergyman was a few roots of taro, or a fowl, or a little bundle of onions. Six hundred couples were united by one minister in three months! I remember, myself, a native gardener coming to us to ask to borrow a paper collar, because he was going to be married.

When Liholiho, Kamehameha II., formally received the first missionaries, he had five queens at his right hand, two of whom were his half-sisters. As the foreign ladies came in, the king turned to the nearest of them, saying that these foreigners wanted to remain in the kingdom and to teach a new religion. "One of their peculiar doctrines is that a man must have but one wife. If they remain, I shall be obliged to send away four of you!" Kamamalu replied, "Let it be so, let them remain and be as you say." But perhaps this queen knew that she was the favourite, for she it was whom he kept as his only wife.

The hearts of the wives of the doctor and the missionaries were naturally drawn out towards the women and the children. Mothers' meetings were not talked of in those days, but they held them all the same, and at the first of these many gathered, bringing their children with them. Queen Kaahumanu came, with little Ruth, and with Kinau was a fine boy, Prince David Kamehameha. "Some of the mothers presented their children, with all the pride of old Roman matrons." Those who had none were requested to rise.

"Why are you childless?" was the question put to these. It was known that few had lost their offspring in a natural way.

A woman held out both hands, crying in tears, "These must answer for me. I have borne eight children, but with these hands I buried them alive, one after another, as soon as they saw the light. I wanted to follow my pleasures, and not to grow old-looking. Oh, that I had one of them back again to comfort me now! If tears and sorrow could restore the dead!" She was followed by others making the same sad confessions of burying alive, of strangling, of smothering, until sobs and tears filled the house.

"Oh," said one, "you have little idea of our heartless depravity, before we had the Word of God. We thought only of preserving our youth and beauty, following the train of our king and chiefs, singing, dancing, and being merry. When old we expected to be cast aside, and being neglected, to starve and die, and we only cared for the present pleasures. Such was our darkness."

"The scene was painful," says Mrs. Judd, "We tried to say a few words of consolation and advice, and to commend them to God in prayer. We made arrangements to meet them regularly once a month for instruction in maternal and domestic duties, and returned to our own happy Christian homes, feeling that we had never before realised how much we owe to the Gospel."

A Practical Mission

After my return I related to Pali, my native woman, some of the fearful disclosures made at the meeting. "My mother had ten children," said she; "my brother now with you, and myself, are all that escaped death at her hands. This brother was buried too, but I loved him very much, and determined to save him if I could. I watched my mother and saw where she buried him. As soon as she went away, I ran and dug him up. He was not dead. I ran many miles with him, and kept him hid with some friends a long time. My mother heard of us and tried to get us back, but I kept going from one place to another, and after a while she died. I have always taken care of him until now."

The health of some of the mission party having begun to suffer, Dr. and Mrs. Judd went with others to seek for a health-station in the more bracing parts of the snow-capped mountains. She writes on her way: "Kealakekua is an historical spot. I write this in sight of the very rock where the celebrated Captain Cook was killed, and I have seen the man who ate his heart. He stole it from a tree supposing it to be a swine's heart hung there to dry, and was horrified when he discovered the truth. The Sandwich Islanders never were cannibals. This made him famous, and he is always spoken of as the man who ate Lono's heart. Here I have made the acquaintance of the old queen, Kekupuohi, wife of Kalaniopuu. She was close to Captain Cook when he fell, following her royal husband, whom the English were enticing on board the ship to be detained as a hostage, until a stolen boat should be restored. She says the natives had supposed that Captain Cook was their old god, Lono, returned to visit them. They paid him divine honours, which he must well have understood. Men were sent from the ship, who cut down the fences around their temple. Women visited the ship in great numbers, and husbands grew jealous, and began to distrust these new divinities. A young chief was killed by a shot from one of the ships, while passing in his canoe. There was a great uproar among the people, and when they saw their king about to step into the boat with Captain Cook, an old warrior said: "I do not believe he is a god. I will prick him with my spear, and if he cries out I shall know he is not." He struck him in the back, Cook uttered a cry—the chief gave another thrust—and the great navigator proved

A DIFFICULT LANDING STAGE

to be mortal. These facts were gathered from an eye-witness, who expressed the deepest regret at the sad tragedy.

Just across the bay is the birthplace of Obookaiah, the first native convert to Christianity. He went to America in a whaleship, was taken up and cared for by some benevolent people, who founded the Cornwall school.

When Mr. Ruggles and Dr. Judd returned, having selected a locality for the health-station, Mr. and Mrs. Ruggles, Miss Ward and ourselves embarked in canoes for Kawaihae. Here we were entertained by old John Young, an English runaway sailor, who had been many years on the islands, and had assisted Kamehameha in his conquests. He had married a native woman of rank, has a fine family of sons and daughters, and is considered a chief. He lived in a dirty adobe house, adorned with old, rusty muskets, swords, bayonets, and cartridge boxes. He gave us a supper of goat's meat and fried tato served on old pewter plates, which I was unfortunate enough to see his servant wipe on his red flannel shirt in lieu of a napkin. I was surprised to see how imperfectly Mr. Young spoke the native language. We were sent up a rickety flight of stairs to sleep. I was afraid, and requested Dr. Judd to look around the room carefully for concealed dangers, and he was heartless enough to laugh at me. Sleep was out of the question. I was afraid of the wind which sometimes sweeps down the gorge of the mountain, and got up at midnight, and went down to the grass house of Mrs. Young, which was neat and comfortable. She is a noble woman. She lives in native style. One of the sons is with the king, and the daughters are in the train of the princess."

After twelve prosperous and happy years, death visited the doctor's home, and their eldest, "the son of our strength, our promising beloved Gerrit," was taken.

Hoohano, a young native who was a medical pupil of Dr. Judd's, was much attached to the boy. The night after he died he watched by the body, and whilst watching he composed some native lines, the poetic feeling of which Mrs. Judd says the following translation but poorly renders. Gerrit used to go and sit in Hoohano's room and sing with him. The "occupant of the garden," and "the chief tenant" refer to Gerrit's father, the "tenant resident" to the mother. "Pioneer" refers to a custom the chiefs had when moving from

A Practical Mission

place to place, of sending on messengers to build houses, and make preparations for their arrival.

> Farewell to the beautiful flower of the doctor's garden;
> It has fallen and vanished away.
> The flower that budded first and blossomed fair.
> Its splendour was seen; its fragrance exhaled;
> But the burning sun came and it withered,
> And that beautiful blossom has fallen.
> The occupant of the garden then wondered
> That a certain flower should have fallen.
> He sought it, but found it not again; it was gone;
> It had perished; it had mingled with the dust.
> Alas! what pity for the flower plants,
> Which grow up well, and lo! they are withered.
> All the flowers bowed their heads smelling the fragrance;
> They stood around in great sorrow.
> Alas! alas! O my blossom that has fallen!
> The chief tenant inquired of his landlord,
> What thinkest thou concerning this flower,
> Which thou didst plant in my border?
> The Lord replied, "I have taken away the image of all its glory;
> Its hut has fallen and is mingled with the dust."
> How beautifully did the plant flourish;
> Great compassion for the tenant resident;
> Mourning and searching with great lamentation;
> Whither, O Gerrit, hast thou gone?
> When wilt thou return to thy birthmates?
> Alone hast thou gone in the way that is lonely;
> Thou hast gone a stranger in an unknown path,

O Gerrit! Gerrit! behold we all
Are stricken flowers and soon shall fall.
Where art thou? Go, thou, and be a pioneer to welcome us.
O Gerrit! Thou goest at the pleasure of thy Lord,
And none can forbid thy design; go, thou,
Travel on until thou art wholly gone along the silent pathway;
Ascend the ladder of God's kingdom,
And pass within the glorious walls of Jerusalem,
And enter into the peace of God's kingdom.
Thou art singing hymns with good angels,
And never ceasing is thy employment there.
O Gerrit! Gerrit! Deeply we mourn that we cannot behold thee;
For ever hast thou gone from our sight,
And wilt return hither no more.

One of Mrs. Judd's little daughters wrote as a school composition a very pretty description of a native servant they had. "Old Hannah is nearly forty years old, but cannot tell exactly, as the natives reckon by some event that took place—not by the years. She says she was a little girl when old Kamehameha I. died; that she belonged to the train of Queen Kamamalu, who died in England. She used to be a skilful dancer, and now sometimes when she is talking very earnestly, she forgets herself and steps off to the right and left, gesturing with her hands as if she were dancing.

"Kuaole, her husband, is very stupid about learning to read, but is a very good farmer; he takes care of the garden, plants taro and sweet potatoes. Old Hannah orders him about as if he were her servant, and he generally does as she wishes, though sometimes he growls a little. They sleep in their own house, a little distance from us, but always manage to be here in season for a warm breakfast, particularly a bowl of hot tea or coffee, of which they are very fond.

"They are both Church members, and Hannah spends a great deal of her time in looking after straying Church members, and getting people out to meeting. She is never tired of walking and talking. She is a great flatterer, and when she wants any particular favour of my mother, she always begins by telling her how somebody has praised her children, or said how young and good-looking she was, and how much all the chiefs had always admired her looks and skill. She takes care of the poultry, and does some housework, is very fond of planting and watering the flowers.

"She is a leader of the fashions among her class, and often comes to see us to contrive some new style of dress for them. She likes red or blue basques, with white skirts. When she sweeps the house she always gathers out every fragment of silk, ribbon, or bright coloured cloth, and makes them into trimming for her bonnet.

"A few months ago she heard of the death of her father in Hawaii, and that he had left her his fortune. Accordingly, on December 18 she bade adieu to all the family with many tears, and sailed one hundred and fifty miles across the rough channel after her fortune.

"We did not hear anything from her until a week ago, when her husband came in and said Hannah had returned, but could not come ashore till we had sent her a dress to wear, as hers was worn out. The dress was sent, and she soon made her appearance. She related her adventures as follows: The schooner made a long passage of twelve days, when she landed at Kawaihae, where the old temple was built in the days of Kamehameha I., and where old Mr. Young lived. She went on foot up to Waimea, where Mr. Lyons lives, fifteen miles. Then she travelled through the deep forest of Mahiki, and down the great pali to Hamakua, where her fortune was. She obtained it. It was a few goats, one pig, two ducks, and one turkey.

"She drove them a long distance, but one goat was troublesome, so she despatched it (she did not say how). After that the rest went along quietly, and she reached Kawaihae, and embarked with two ducks and a turkey, leaving the rest to come by the next vessel.

"The schooner made a long voyage down, and she was very sick. She ate one of the ducks during the passage, so all she had to show for her trouble and fatigue was one duck and one turkey."

CHAPTER VII

KAMEHAMEHA III., HIS ADVISERS, AND HIS AGGRESSORS

In studying the past history of Hawaii, as well as in my own observations during our time there, I was struck with the prominent part played by women. They seem, in fact, as a whole, to have more decision of character and more intelligence than the men. In this later period there had been Kapiolani; Kaahumanu, the Queen-Regent; Keopuolani, the queen-mother who established the Lahaina mission; and the evil Liliha, wife of Boki. After his fatal voyage in quest of sandal-wood, which ended in the king's brig being lost with all on board, Liliha succeeded Boki, as Governess of Oahu, besides helping Kinau, another notable woman leader, in the management of affairs in Oahu for nine months.

Liliha was the unworthy daughter of Hoapili.

At one time, when she nearly caused a civil war, the fine old chief settled matters by sailing to Honolulu, and, proceeding to her dwelling—she had filled the fort on Punch Bowl with armed men—he simply told her he wished her to go home with him to Lahaina. She was wise, and went.

Kaahumanu had appointed Kinau, a daughter of Kamehameha, as her successor in the office of Regent. She was a discreet and good woman, and half-sister to the young king. Her official title was Kaahumanu II. She had married a chief of great ability, and two of her sons afterwards came to the throne. Unfortunately, after the death of his guardian Kaahumanu, the king came more and more under the influence of Liliha's party and of the unprincipled British Consul, Charlton. He formed a company of fast-living young men, who took the name of "Hulumanu"—*i.e.*, bird-feathers. Kaomi, a renegade Tahitian teacher, was one of the worst of these. He was called familiarly by a name signifying "the engrafted king." This man treated Kinau, the Regent, with contempt, and even arrogated to himself her authority. Under this evil influence all laws were ignored, excepting those against theft, sedition, and murder. Hoapili, the fine old chief of Maui, was the foster-father of the king, but he tried in vain to restrain him.

Still, Kamehameha was not wholly given over to evil ways. At heart he was convinced that it would be well if he could follow in the leadings of his teachers, whom he always respected and upheld by word of mouth, even when he found it difficult to carry out their precepts.

To quote again from Mrs. Judd's diary, she wrote in 1829:—

"After many months of hard labour our new thatched church is completed. Several hundred men at a time have been engaged in putting on the thatch under the superintendence of Governor Boki, who has set overseers, sword in hand, at the different portions of the work. The men chatter while at work like so many meadow larks, and their voices are sufficiently confused to remind one of what the scene might have been at Babel's tower. The church has a neat pulpit of native mahogany (koa), a glazed window behind, draped with crimson damask furnished by Kaahumanu. Upholstering is a new business. We had some idea of festoons, but knew not how to arrange them so

Kamehameha III.

as to produce the proper effect, for we were without patterns and had no one to teach us. The young king was anxious to have it as grand as possible, as it was his chapel. We did our best, and what more is required of mortals?

"The king, his royal sister, and a large number of the chiefs from the other islands were present at the dedication. Kaahumanu made a very interesting address to the people, and to the surprise of all present the king followed with a speech and a prayer. He not only dedicated the house to the worship of the only living and true God, but solemnly then and there consecrated his kingdom to the Lord Jesus Christ. The princess and her maids of honour led the choir and the chant, 'O come let us sing unto the Lord,' which was sung in excellent taste. Governer Boki made a great display of soldiers, dressed in new suits purchased for the occasion, augmenting the public debt some thousands of dollars. He appeared restless and ill at ease.

"I record another anecdote of Kaahumanu; the incident occurred a few weeks before the dedication. Mrs. Bingham, Miss Ward and myself were spending the day with her at her rustic country-seat in Manoa valley. As we were seated at our sewing, Kaahumanu very kindly inquired what we thought of wearing at the dedication of the new church. Without waiting for an answer, she added, 'It is my wish that we dress alike; I have made a selection that pleases me, and it only waits your approval.' She ordered the woman in waiting to bring in the material; it was heavy satin, striped pink, white and blue.

"She fixed her scrutinising eyes upon us as we examined and commented upon it in our own language. As we hesitated in the approval, 'What fault has it?' she hastily inquired. I replied, 'No fault; it is very beautiful for you who are a queen, but we are missionaries, supported by the churches and the earnings of the poor, and such expensive material is not suitable for us.'

"'I give it to you,' she replied, 'not to the church, nor the poor.'

"'Foreigners will be present,' we said, 'who will perhaps make ill-natured remarks.'

"'Foreigners!' said she, 'do you mean those in town who tear off calico?' (meaning the salesmen in the shops). 'What do you care for their opinions? It does not concern them;

you should not heed what they say' We declined still further the acceptance as we should not ourselves feel comfortable in such unaccustomed attire. She looked disappointed and displeased, and ordered the woman to put it out of sight, adding, 'If it is not proper for good people to wear good things, I do not know what they are made for.' We were sorry to oppose her wishes, and she was taciturn all the afternoon. As we were about to take leave at evening, she resumed her cheerful manner, and asked what we would like to wear on the forthcoming occasion. We thanked her, and said we would like to make something very handsome for her, but we should prefer black silk to anything else for ourselves. She made no reply, but bade us an affectionate good-night. The next morning we received two rolls of black silk, with an order to make her dress exactly like ours."

When Kaahumanu felt that her end was near she expressed a desire to be taken to the beautiful and secluded valley of Manoa, which is near Honolulu, requesting the doctor and Mrs. Judd to go with her. A bed of sweet scented maile and leaves of ginger was prepared, over which was spread a covering of velvet, and in this she laid herself down to die! ... "She was gentle as a lamb, and treated her attendants with great tenderness; 'Do sit down, you are very tired, I make you weary,' she said often." The New Testament, in native, was just then in the press, so a copy was hastily finished, bound in red morocco, with her name in gilt embossed letters on the cover. She looked carefully through to assure herself that it was complete, then she wrapped it in her handkerchief and laid it on her bosom, clasped her hands over it, and contentedly closed her eyes. A little later she asked for her teachers, Mr. and Mrs. Bingham; "I am going," she said, "where the mansions are ready." To some words of theirs she replied, "Yes, I shall go to Him and be comforted." A faint "Aloha" —"love to you"—and a gentle hand pressure, and, says Mrs. Judd, "the throbbings of that affectionate heart were stilled for ever."

In 1833 Kamehameha III.—the young king—declared his determination to put his minority at an end and "to take into his hands the power of life and death and the undivided sovereignty." All feared that he would now set Liliha or the low caste Tahitian in the place of Kinau, and that a civil war would follow. A great assembly of chiefs was called, and the latter as she came in saluted her half-brother, saying, "We cannot war with the word of God between us."

Then the king made his speech; after which, lifting his hand, as was the custom, to appoint the one who was to be second in the kingdom, he declared Kinau to be premier. Afterwards he was asked how he came to do this, and his reply was remarkable. He said simply, "Very strong is the kingdom of God." A year later Hoapili and the other chiefs destroyed every distillery on Oahu. Kaomi, the Tahitian, retired for a time to a small hut at Lahaina, and then died on his way to Honolulu.

The king also adopted Kinau's third son, Alexander Liho-liho, as his heir and successor.

The child was born soon after he had asserted himself as Sovereign. The king visited his sister Kinau, just after his birth, and after some kindly expressions "he looked affectionately at the babe, and stuck in the thatch of Kinau's dwelling as he left a slip of paper with these four words, 'This child is mine,' a way of telling his true and patient guardian that her boy should be his special charge."

The babe was carried in a blanket to the palace, where a set of nurses and servants were appointed for his care. The king had no child; two fine boys he had lost in their infancy. A state carriage in the shape of a hand cart, drawn and accompanied by sixteen men arrived every day at the doctor's door to convey Mrs. Judd to the palace to wash and dress the royal infant. The clothes she took from her own family store of baby linen. A number of native nurses assisted at the baby's toilet. This child was Kamehameha IV., the husband of Queen Emma.

The first English newspaper was printed in this year under the name of *The Sandwich Island Gazette*, and sugar, silk and cotton plantations were commenced in the islands.

In 1837 the king was married to his favourite, Kalama, a bright young girl of not very high rank.

Under Kinau's influence, the king and the chiefs forbade the teaching of the Roman Catholic religion, and the unfortunate persecution of Catholics had followed. It was mainly owing to Mr. Richards that the king issued in 1839 an edict of toleration, and two women who had been confined in irons in the fort were released. Captain Laplace, who arrived in a French frigate in 1839, issued a manifesto, saying that his Majesty, the King of the French had sent him "to put an end, either by force or by persuasion, to the ill-treatment to which the French had been victims . . . they must now comprehend that to tarnish the Catholic religion with the name of idolatry, and to expel the French under that absurd pretext was to offer an insult to France and her Sovereign." Captain Laplace then demanded the following concessions under threat—in case of non-fulfilment—of immediate war; the king's secretary being kept on board the frigate as a hostage.

Hostilities were postponed for a few days to allow the king, who was absent on Maui, to arrive in Honolulu. On the following Sunday morning, after the king returned, Captain Laplace, accompanied by one hundred and fifty men, with fixed bayonets and a band of music, marched to a building that belonged to the king, and held there a grand military mass, the services concluding with the "Te Deum." Next morning, early, the king was coerced into signing a "convention," of which two important stipulations were: first, that "no Frenchman shall be tried for any crime, except by a jury of foreign residents nominated by the French Consul, and the latter, that French merchandise, especially wine or brandy, shall not be prohibited, nor pay a higher duty than five per cent. ad valorem."

Then the *Artémise* left, to the great relief of the natives. Poor Hawaii! intoxicating and, to the natives, debasing liquors forced on her, not only by English convicts but by a civilised nation; and a priesthood, too, against her will.

One of the clauses, however, in a Declaration of Rights which was signed by the king, when the draft of the first Constitution was drawn up in the Hawaiian language in 1839, was, "All men of every religion shall be protected in worshipping Jehovah and serving him according to their own understanding," and much noble work has been done in the islands by the Roman Catholics. The corner-stone of the large native church of Kawaiahao, in which, in my time, the present ex-queen Liliuo-kalani, then Mrs. Dominis, wife of Governor Dominis of Oahu, often led the native choir, was laid in 1839. The different chiefs agreed each of them to supply so many hundred blocks of coral stone, which their retainers hewed out of the coral reef for that purpose. They were ever gratefully mindful of the education they received from the early mission. This church was finished in 1842, when a great effort was made to pledge the people to temperance. Fourteen hundred children formed a sort of band of hope at the time, the king also taking a pledge of total abstinence; his friends found it very difficult, however, to keep him from his gambling haunts. The love of games of chance was in the Hawaiian blood.

A boarding school for children of royalty and for the high chiefs' families, where the young princes especially, being freed from their foolish and flattering dependants—who ruined them by the way in which they pandered to their wishes—could be under good influences, was now founded, the native Governor Kekuanaoa helping most generously in erecting the buildings, whilst other chiefs did their share. Kinau's children were pupils there; in fact the four future kings were trained at this school; and Mr. Richards, having been appointed Minister of Public Instruction, was made director also of this establishment.

I fancied often that there was a good deal of jealousy shown by the French with regard to the Americans. A saying of one of the French consuls who spoke poor English was often quoted, in my time, in Honolulu. He had been wont to observe confidentially to one of his English friends, " The American peeps (people) think they are a very big peeps—but they can *not*." This was accompanied by a shrug and a gesture expressive of infinite contempt of the powers of that " big peeps."

In 1840 the British Consul, Mr. Charlton, had begun to make grievances, having an evident desire to get the islands annexed to Great Britain. The chiefs had granted him government land for a consulate, and also another piece for an official residence. He put in later a claim for a large block adjoining the former, saying that the late Governor Kalanimoku, since dead, had given him a lease of it, dated 1826, for two hundred and ninety-nine years. It is believed by good judges that the deed was a forgery or that a signature had been obtained through ignorance of its contents. The king said that the land belonged to Kaahumanu, and now was the property of her heirs.

Harassed on all sides through foreign relationships, Kamehameha and his advisers felt that a formal recognition of the independence of his kingdom from the Great Powers had become a necessity; but even here the British Consul's greed and duplicity caused complications

Charlton left suddenly for London by Mexico, sending a threatening letter to the king that he had appointed a gentleman as acting consul, one who was also an open advocate of British annexation, and an enemy of the Governor of Oahu. The king declined to acknowledge the appointment. Mr. Richards and Haalilio, the king's secretary, proceeded to Washington, where they had interviews with Daniel Webster, then Secretary of State, from whom they received a document which recognised the independence of the Hawaiian kingdom, declaring it as "the sense of the government of the United States that the government of the Sandwich Islands ought to be respected, that no Power ought to take possession of the islands, either as a conquest or for the purpose of colonisation, and that no Power ought to seek for any undue control over the existing government, or any exclusive privileges or preferences in matters of commerce."

President Tyler confirmed this expression in his message to Congress in December 1842.

The envoys then went on to London, but meanwhile Charlton on reaching Mexico misrepresented matters to Lord George Paulet, who was in command there of the *Carysfort*;

and besides this Mr. Simpson, the consul in charge, sent despatches from Honolulu pretending that the property and persons of the British residents were in danger—so that Rear-Admiral Thomas ordered the *Carysfort* to proceed to Honolulu in order to inquire into the state of things.

Mr. Simpson's uncle, Sir George Simpson, who was a governor in the service of the Hudson Bay Company, had been in Honolulu and become interested in the natives and their king. He had indeed offered to lend them ten thousand pounds in cash to help them out of present difficulties. and it had been through his advice that the king's commissioners had been sent to the foreign Powers. This gentleman was in London when these arrived, and he helped them greatly. At first Lord Aberdeen, then Secretary of State for Foreign Affairs, declined to receive them as Ministers from an independent State, nor would he negotiate a treaty. He said Kamehameha did not govern, he was "exclusively under the influence of Americans to the detriment of British interests," and he did not admit that the United States Government had yet fully recognised their independence.

Sir George and Mr. Richards then went to Brussels, where King Leopold I. received them with great courtesy, promising his influence on their side, which they considered valuable on account of his close relationship to the English and French royalties. In France, M. Guizot received the envoys very kindly, and promised to help in every way to promote the independence of their government.

On their return to London, through Sir George Simpson's true representation of the Hawaiian position, Lord Aberdeen gave an assurance that the Consul, Mr. Charlton, should be removed, and that the independence of the Sandwich Islands should be recognised by Her Majesty's Government, and also the rule of its Sovereign; but "insisting on the perfect equality of all foreigners in the islands before the law," &c.

Mr. Richards and the chief Haalilio now returned to the Continent to obtain a formal recognition from France. Unfortunately a Mr. Brinsmade, who was associated with the great firm of Ladd and Co., sugar planters, on the island of Kauai, who had obtained from the king a great tract of land for their purposes, met them here, and with him they negotiated a contract with "the Belgian Company of Colonisation," a wealthy body in which the King of the Belgians was a stock-holder.

In the meantime Lord George Paulet, completely won over by Mr. Simpson, had arrived at Honolulu, where he arrogantly withheld the usual salutes. He also refused to treat with the king through his agent, Dr. Judd, and sent him a peremptory letter of demands with a threat that if they were not complied with by four o'clock of the following afternoon "immediate coercive steps would be taken." This was late in the evening.

Next morning the frigate was cleared and her battery brought to bear on the town. Some English families took refuge on a brig outside the harbour, and the American and others placed their valuables on board the *Boston*.

At first the king and chiefs determined to resist, and before four o'clock they sent a letter to Lord George Paulet, explaining that their envoys had been sent to Europe, with power to settle the difficulties that had arisen, and that some of his demands were "calculated to seriously embarrass this feeble government by contravening the laws established for the benefit of all." The king, however, declared he would agree to comply with them under protest, appealing later for justice to the British Government.

Salutes were then exchanged between the fort and the frigate, and two days later the king was received with royal honours on the *Carysfort*. He was, however, met with unreasonable claims, and outrageous demands, treated with insolence, and allowed no chance of consultation with his advisers.

Kamehameha's patience was exhausted and his heart well-nigh broken. "I will not die piecemeal; they may cut off my head at once," he cried, after a night of thought and prayer, with his chiefs "Let them take what they please; I will give no more."

"Dr. Judd then advised him to forestall the intended seizure of the islands by a temporary cession to Lord Paulet, pending an appeal to the British Goverment." Other foreign residents urged him to cede his kingdom, jointly, to France and the United States. An Act of cession was offered him to this effect, but he refused to sign it. Next day, preliminaries were arranged with Lord George Paulet, and two days later, a provisional cession was signed by the king and his council. By a curious coincidence, it was the forty-ninth anniversary of the day of Kamehameha I.'s cession to Vancouver in 1794, when he and the chiefs in council with him had, of their own accord, placed their country under the protection of Great Britain. That was a cession, however, which was never ratified by the English Government.

The flag of Hawaii was lowered and the British colours were hoisted over the fort by a lieutenant of the *Carysfort*. English marines marched into the fort whilst their band played "God save the Queen" and "Isle of beauty, fare thee well."

The king's Hawaiian address was pathetic. "Where are you, chiefs, people, and commons from my ancestors, and people from foreign lands! Hear ye! I make known to you that I am in perplexity by reason of difficulties into which I have been brought without cause. Wherefore I have given away the life of our land, hear ye! But my rule over you, my people, and your privileges, will continue, for I hope that the life of the land will be restored when my conduct shall be justified."

Lord George then proclaimed that the government should be carried on, so far as natives were concerned, by the king and chiefs, and that of foreigners by a commission, Dr. Judd being appointed as the king's representative, Lord George, his first lieutenant, and another, a Mr. Mackay, making up the number. The king retired then with his retinue to Lahaina on the island of Maui, and a "secret correspondence was kept up between him and his officers at Honolulu, by means of canoes manned by trusty retainers."

All prisoners under arrest were set free, and vice became open and rampant, under the new *régime*. Dr. Judd resigned, as did Mr. Mackay; so Lord George Paulet and his lieutenant were masters of the situation. At Lahaina, at this time, on the first anniversary of its temperance society, a large quantity of wine and spirits which had been lying for a year, untouched, in the cellar of the king was emptied into the sea, a fact that spoke strongly as to his desire to keep sober and to have his wits about him.

The commission—save the mark—enlisted a small standing army of natives, whom they dubbed the "Queen's Regiment."

The men were commanded and drilled by British officers. The king protested against the expense incurred in this and other ways, and Dr. Judd, fearing that the national archives might be seized, hid these in the royal tomb. "There," says Mr. Jarves, in his history, "in this abode of death, surrounded by the former sovereigns of Hawaii and using the coffin of Kaahumanu for a table, for many weeks he nightly found an unsuspected asylum for his labours on behalf of the kingdom."

At last the king forbade Dr. Judd to pay out of the treasury any more money for the support of the regiment, but Lieutenant Frere compelled him to give the money, going to him with his naked sword in hand.

Happily, at this juncture, Rear-admiral Thomas arrived in person and, hardly was his vessel, the *Dublin*, at anchor, before he courteously requested an audience with the king, and the news flew over the islands that he had come to restore their independence. The terms of restoration were, in fact, soon arranged by Admiral Thomas, who declared, in the name of the British Queen, that he did not accept of the provisional cession, adding, "Her Majesty sincerely desires King Kamehameha III. to be treated as an independent Sovereign, leaving the administration of justice in his own hands."

The king signed at the same time with the admiral, a convention, guarding strictly all British interests. To this day the Hawaiians talk of "the good admiral" who gave back to them the life of their land, and the open space where the ceremonies took place, on what was then a bare plain, is still called in memory of him, "Thomas Square."

The natives of the late "Queen's Regiment" went to the king's residence to demand his pardon and to swear an allegiance to him for the future. Kamehameha then attended a thanksgiving service in the great native church, addressing his people there. The present national motto of Hawaii—"the life of the land is perpetuated by righteousness"—comes from the very words which their king used on that occasion.

Until Admiral Thomas could receive the approval of the Home Government of the steps he had taken, he took up his residence on shore in Honolulu. To use Lord Canning's words his just conduct was "marked by great propriety and admirable judgment throughout." Mrs. Judd gives an amusing account of a dinner the doctor and she gave to the king and high chiefs, the English Admiral Thomas, the

American commisioner and the consuls of various nations, about this time.

She says it was a cold water entertainment, the American commissioner being an earnest temperance advocate. She gave it with some misgivings, and it was thought advisable to consult the English admiral as to this beforehand, as it was presumed that "he had never dined without wine in his life before, and probably would be uncomfortable without it." The hosts, however, felt they were pledged to the king and his people on this question.

"The soup was good—the fish, the finest and fattest from the royal ponds. The rice and curry were good enough for the Great Mogul. Roast beef, mutton, boned-turkey, ham, ducks, chickens, salads (hot and cold), lobster, game, omelets, patties, puddings, pies, almond pastry, fruit, nuts and raisins, crackers and cheese followed each other in due order, all faultless. But the waiters were slow. It seemed a lifetime between the courses. I tasked my brain for sprightly sayings. The admiral was cheerful, but it was plain he missed his wine. His secretary had cramps in his stomach; cold water always produced that effect on him, and he could eat nothing after his soup. I had half a mind to go to the medicine chest and get a glass of wine for him; but there sat our Sovereign and chiefs, and I would not set wine before them for a kingdom.

"Three hours dragged their slow length along, and the cloth was removed for tea and coffee; but the admiral excused himself, as his hour for an evening walk had arrived. Others followed in haste for antidotes against the cold water that was chilling them. A few remained and made themselves sufficiently merry and agreeable with drinks that 'cheer, but not inebriate.'

"When all the guests had retired, I sat down to reflect, half-mortified, half-vexed. Can it be possible, I thought, that high-bred gentlemen, of intellect and education, are so dependent upon artificial stimulants that they cannot relish a good dinner without them? Are the wit and the fine sayings at the social board of great men nothing but the sparkling effervescence of champagne, and are fine spirits the spirits of the distillery only?

"We were happy to receive afterward the full approval of the admiral, who assured us that such a course was the only proper one, and would secure the happiest results, although he had at first regarded the principle of total abstinence as an ultra measure."

On November 28, 1843, France and Enggland united in a declaration to the effect that: "Her Majesty the Queen of the United Kingdom of Great Britain and Ireland, and His Majesty the King of the French, taking into consideration the existence in the Sandwich Islands of the Government capable of providing for the regularity of its relations with foreign nations, have thought it right to engage reciprocally to consider the Sandwich Islands as an independent State, and never to take possession either directly or under the title of a Protectorate, or under any other form, of any part of the territory of which they are composed. . . ."

And so the Hawaiian kingdom now ranked as one of the civilised nations; and its envoys returned to the United States in 1844 where they received a despatch informing them that the President regarded the statement of Mr. Webster and the appointment of a commissioner "as a full recognition on the part of the United States of the independence of the Hawaiian Government." It was now that General Miller was acting as Consul for Great Britain, and with him was Mr. R. C. Wyllie who made

Hawaii his home for twenty years, employing there the results of his learning, and great energy and tact in its service. He came of a Scottish family which has been noted for the enterprise and tact of many of its members.

Poor Haalilio who had long been in feeble health died at sea on his way home, and his remains were placed in the royal tomb with sincere mourning on the part of all the Honolulu residents.

A time of material prosperity now set in. Fifty whaleships lay at one time off Lahaina, and during 1845 about five hundred touched at the islands. The moral influence was hurtful, however.

I have alluded several times to the state carriages, which up to the year 1847, consisted of hand-carts gaily painted. The king had lately bought from Pomare, Queen of Tahiti, a carriage which had been presented to her by Queen Victoria. She never recovered from the humiliation which she suffered when the French practically took possession of her country. She was very independent, and declared herself too poor to keep up so grand a means of conveyance, so it had been sent to Honolulu for sale. At a great feast of the natives given by the Governor and Paki, the High Chamberlain, the king and queen rode in it for the first time. It was drawn by four beautiful, grey horses, their harness gaily decorated.

In consequence of the more settled condition of things in Hawaii, there was great material progress for some years, and many improvements were made in the public buildings of Honolulu. The first road for horses over the pass by the Nuuanu precipice, was opened now, a great help to the commerce of the island. More sugar plantations were started, and the first coffee plantation was begun at Hanalei, on Kauai. They found also that they could raise wheat in Makawao.

The discovery of gold in California in 1848, was a great help to the industries of the islands. A party of men left Honolulu for the gold-diggings, and a market was opened there for Hawaiian products which was a great factor in the development of the country.

The Belgian Company not having carried out the contract which they had made with the firm of Ladd and Co., that house failed in business, and their property was sold, by order of the Government, for the benefit of the creditors. This was, in fact, a blessing for the country, as the execution of the Belgian contract would have been a very bad thing for the native race, and the company would have monopolised in time all foreign trade.

In 1848 a full-length portrait of Louis Philippe was presented to Kamehameha III. It came with the French corvette *Sarcelle*, with Mr. Dillon, a new French Consul. Twelve men of the *Sarcelle* were required to carry it up, a body of marines was appointed to guard it, a band of music accompanied it, and there was a salute of twenty-one guns. The wife of the Consul and others followed it in carriages, the portrait, in a massive gilt frame, being wrapped in the French national flag. Bishop Maigret, with his clergy and all the French residents, walked behind. Another salute was fired from Punch Bowl on its arrival at the Palace, where, as Mrs. Judd tells us, the king, queen, young chiefs from the royal school, Government officers, and ladies and gentlemen stood on the steps to receive the portrait. The Lord Chamberlain, assisted with a few men, succeeded in getting it safely into the reception room, and in the evening the king opened the palace to any callers who wished to come and look at the picture, which gift had caused great gratification to the royal family, and indeed to all the people.

Just ten days after they received the much valued portrait of Louis Philippe, that king abdicated and fled in disguise.

For some years, under the influence of his best friends, Kamehameha had abstained from all stimulants; unfortunately, all these negotiations with outsiders caused him to fall back again into excesses at times. Under unwise advice, wine was introduced at the king's table at the public dinners. The lady I have before often quoted tells us that this gave them all great uneasiness.

Some of the Honolulu residents were not much enchanted with the opening of the gold-fields in California, we are told, "old blankets, cloaks, pea-jackets, anything in fact was shipped to the coast, the market threatened to be stripped of its food supplies, and they began to fear nothing would be left to them but fish and poi."

Mr. Dillon, the new French Consul, was not a man of tact. He soon began to quarrel with his predecessor and with Mr. Wyllie, and, in fact, undid all the good results of the last five years' work. Grievances of all kinds he manufactured, and his chief grounds of complaint were that the duty on French brandy was too high, and that the English language had more favour shown to it than that of the French! So much bad blood grew out of this that Admiral de Tromelin, in the French frigate *Poursuivante*, arrived at Honolulu in 1849, and was joined there by the *Gassendi*, from Tahiti. Ten demands, which had been drawn up by Mr. Dillon, were sent in a peremptory despatch to the king by the admiral, and the Government was only allowed three days in which to make a satisfactory reply, the admiral threatening that if these were not acceded to he would cancel the existing treaty and "employ the means at his disposal to obtain a complete reparation." The Hawaiian Government could not see its way to granting all these demands, so an armed force was landed, with two field pieces, scaling ladders, &c., with which they took possession of an empty fort. They also took possession of the custom house and other Government buildings, and seized the king's yacht, as well as seven merchant vessels. In spite of this the Government preserved order in the town, and no French citizen was molested in any way.

For ten days they occupied the position, all business being interrupted; no coasting vessels were allowed to leave, and any arriving were at once taken and anchored under the guns of the *Gassendi*. The Hawaiian fort was dismantled, the guns spiked and broken, the magazine opened, and the powder poured into the sea. The Governor's house was wrecked, all his curios, &c., being destroyed.

The British and American Consuls had, of course, protested against these proceedings. Later, some of his acts were disavowed by the French Government, but incalculable mischief had been done. Mr. Dillon was soon afterwards appointed to the office of French Consul-General in San Francisco. The king and the counsel now resolved to send Dr. Judd as a special envoy to France, and in his charge went also the two young princes, the king's nephews, who were afterwards his successors.

Unfortunately Mr. Dillon had preceded them to Paris, and had managed to secure the confidence of the Minister of Foreign Affairs. They remained in Paris ten weeks, but were not able to negotiate a satisfactory treaty. In England the young princes were treated with great hospitality; they were greatly admired among

Kamehameha III.

the aristocracy for the good breeding which they showed and their ease in society. "And where did they acquire Court manners?" asked one great lady. "We have a little Court of our own," replied Dr. Judd.

They met Lord George Paulet and Lieutenant Frere, whose arbitrary measures had caused so much sorrow in Hawaii; but both men were very cordial, and evidently wished to forget all that was disagreeable. At Buckingham Palace Lord Palmerston introduced the party to Prince Albert. The Queen had retired from public life just then for a short season.

Dr. Judd wrote home: "I told Prince Albert that the King of the Sandwich Islands had sent me to Europe to obtain justice from France for injuries received, and that these young princes accompanied me in order to be benefited by foreign travel; that our visit to Paris had been unsuccessful, and we now sought the aid of the greatest diplomat in Europe (designating Lord Palmerston).

"His Royal Highness replied, he hoped it was not too late to come between us and France. He made inquiries about the islands, our journey, &c. When we bowed ourselves out, His Royal Highness gave orders that Dr.

Bridges Taylor, a gentleman connected with the Foreign Office, should attend us to Windsor Castle, and show us all we wished to see in London."

The basis of a new treaty with England was agreed upon with Lord Palmerston. A similar treaty was concluded with the United States, and both came into effect in 1851.

Of Daniel Webster, Dr. Judd wrote that he was "more formal, cold and stiff than any lord in Europe."

France still made difficulties. There is an amusing touch in one of Dr. Judd's letters from Paris. Guizot said to him, "Might not the affairs be arranged by arbiters?" suggesting the King of Belgium. "He said the King of Denmark did not know much, and the King of Prussia was young and flippant. The Queen of England might appoint a person, but the Greek question was an obstacle, as the French were chosen to mediate." This referred to some late difficulties of Greece with England. "It is easy to see," added Dr. Judd, "that the Greek question, in which France is chosen umpire, makes it a delicate matter for England to interfere in our difficulties, and coerce the French, either at the Sandwich Islands or

Tahiti. I learned a diplomatic maxim in England, which is worth recording : 'Never tell a lie—*and strictly avoid the truth.*'"

Mr. Perrin was now sent to the islands as Commissioner, and the corvette *Sérieuse* remained in port three months. He again presented the same ten demands that Mr. Dillon had made, although one important claim had been paid in full. The result of a month's useless discussion was that the king and Premier placed the Islands provisionally under the protection of the United States, until "their relations with France should be placed upon a footing compatible with the king's rights as an independent Sovereign, and with his treaty engagements with other nations. The result of this was that Mr. Perrin soon discovered that he could reduce the difficulties of his Government to two points—those regarding the liberty of Catholic worship, and the trade in spirits. Nothing more was ever heard of the other demands.

So far as I remember, it was this Mr. Perrin who used to express his contempt of the American nation, who thought themselves "A very great peeps."

During the close of Kamehameha III.'s

reign, small-pox wrought fearful ravages in the Islands. It is supposed to have been brought from California to Honolulu, in some hundred chests of old clothing which had been brought for auction to the town. The deaths through small-pox amounted to nearly three thousand.

During 1853 and 1854 there was an agitation in favour of annexation to the United States. Both the American mission party, however, and the Roman Catholic mission opposed the project, thinking that its effects on the native race would not be good. The poor king, who was getting tired of demands made upon him by foreign Powers, and by ill-conditioned people in his own country, was greatly in favour of it; the great decrease in the population, the falling off in the numbers of chiefs and other dangers made him feel timid, besides which, he had begun to relapse into the evil habits of his youth. Mr. Wyllie, and Mr. Gregg, the American Minister, were occupied for a considerable time trying to do what was best for all parties, and during the same year Kamehameha died, being only in his forty-second year. He was greatly loved, and his memory is still dear to the Hawaiians. He had granted them a liberal constitution, and had brought about important changes for their good in the land system.

Besides being body physician to the Queen-Regent and her son Kamehameha III., Dr. Judd was, interpreter and recorder to the Government, and later, Secretary of State for Foreign Affairs, and *de facto* Minister of the Interior. After seventeen arduous years, failing health had compelled him to give up the seals of the Foreign Office, and these were transferred to Mr. R. C. Wyllie.

Reverting to the disputes with France and her claims, Dr. Judd tells us that the contest was closed in 1857 by " Mr. Wyllie yielding to France the long contested items of the treaty, and accepting in place of indemnity for the 100,000 dollars damages, a few French 'nicknacks.' " It is only fair to state, however, that a sum of 2000 dollars which had been exacted by Laplace had been restored by Rear-Admiral Hamelin in 1846.

The Americans make a point of the fact that they had, through their missions, taught the people, and practically civilised the islands, many years before English and German merchants began to arrive, and Mr. Wyllie seems to have been the first British resident who had any authorised official part in the Government affairs. We hear so much from well-meaning, as well as merely sentimental folks, about the dealings of the white man with his dark-skinned brother, that a *bonâ fide* account of the way in which an American and Scottish gentleman became factors in Hawaiian history, such as is given in Mr. A. P. Judd's "Honolulu Sketches" is most valuable.

The Land Commission was entirely the idea of Dr. Judd. It was first employed for a year or two upon the claims of foreigners especially. The claims of the natives could not be established on any solid basis until the old feudal system was broken up, as this allowed to the king, the chiefs and the people, an interest in the soil, the tenure of each being subject to the will of his superior. In vain the king and chiefs had endeavoured, during two years, to make a division among themselves which would enable each estate to own some land independently. None but Dr. Judd had the knowledge or the strength of mind to act with authority and to the point. He offered to cut this Gordian knot, if only he might himself appoint and choose a commission to work with him. Endless were the obstacles raised, and the bitternesses caused at first; but the division, when effected, was as just as it could have been, and it proved of immense value to the nation. The Mahele book, or Book of Division, records all the lands of the kingdom, with releases of the lands surrendered on either side.

The appointment of the Scotchman, Mr. Wyllie, as Minister, was also due to the American Dr. Judd's influence. He seems, in all things, to have had the good of his adopted country at heart, and to have acted as a good steward to the king who trusted in him.

CHAPTER VIII

PRINCE ALEXANDER, PRINCE LOT, AND LUNALILO

ALEXANDER LIHOLIHO, the fourth Kamehameha, was twenty-one years of age when he came to the throne in 1855. He was brilliantly clever, a great student of English history, and very ambitious to reign as a constitutional king. The idea of annexation with America was now given up, and instead a treaty of reciprocity was concluded, by which Hawaiian sugar, coffee, wool, hides, &c., were to be admitted into the United States free of duty. This treaty was, however, not ratified at Washington. Mr. Perrin was propitiated by an act which reduced the duty on brandy to three dollars a gallon; the new treaty with France was ratified, and Mr. Perrin presented the king with various silver articles of value and a Sèvres dinner

THE DOWAGER QUEEN EMMA

UNIV. OF
CALIFORNIA

service from the Emperor Napoleon III., these being some of the nick-nacks already alluded to.

The year of his accession, the king married Emma Rooke, a grand-daughter of the English sailor John Young; her mother Fanny Young had a sister who was married to an English physician, Dr. Rooke, a resident in Honolulu, and Emma was adopted in her childhood by the Doctor, taking his name. Through her mother ranking with the high chiefs, she had been educated at their school, where she had always distinguished herself by her talents and great industry.

Partly owing to the good impression produced during the visit of the princes to England and no doubt still more to the influence of Queen Emma, Kamehameha IV. showed from the first a strong partiality for everything that was English. In 1859, through Mr. Wyllie, the Hawaiian Consul in London was requested to make known to the Church of England the desire of the king and queen that a clergyman should be settled in Honolulu, as Chaplain to the Royal Family. They guaranteed a certain sum towards his support, and would give a site for a church. The king himself wrote on the subject to

Queen Victoria. An Anglican mission to the islands was organised, and a first Bishop of Honolulu was consecrated. This was the Rev. T. N. Staley, D.D. The king himself translated the English Book of Common Prayer into the Hawaiian language, and wrote a preface to it.

Queen Emma had given birth to a son whose title was officially declared to be "the Prince of Hawai," but unfortunately he died from brain fever when he was four years old, and the king, who was a very tender-hearted man, and had centred all his hopes on his little son, never recovered from the blow. He retired to a residence in the country, carrying on there his works of translation, which were exceedingly good. But he never recovered from the shock of his son's death, and died himself the following year at the age of twenty-nine. The Queen's Hospital was one of the good works which he inaugurated, and many important public improvements were effected during his reign. The Anglican Mission established the Iolani College for boys, and St. Andrew's Priory for girls, and the foundations for the present cathedral were laid.

In 1855 and 1856 there were two great

eruptions of Mauna Loa. It seemed, during one of these, after a stream of lava, in some places over two miles wide had flowed for fifteen months, as though the town of Hilo would be destroyed. Fortunately the flow ceased within eight miles of the town. In 1859 again another eruption took place on the northern side of the mountain; the fissure was about ten thousand feet above the sea. It reached the sea in eight days and filled up a great fish-pond which had been constructed by Kamehameha the Great, at Kiholo. During seven months this lava continued to flow.

Prince Lot, Kamehameha V., began to reign in November 1863. There is little to tell of him except that he was a firm ruler, whose decision of character enabled him to keep together the various elements in his Government. He made a tour of the islands, attended by Mr. Wyllie whom he retained in his Cabinet, together with Mr. C. C. Harris, an American lawyer, and Mr. C. de Varigny, who had been secretary to the French consul, whilst an Englishman, Dr. Hutchinson, became Minister of the Interior.

Kamehameha V., when dying, foresaw the troubles so soon to beset Hawaii. "What will become of my poor country?" he cried. "Queen Emma I do not trust, Lunalilo is a drunkard, Kalakaua is a fool!"

An important feature of his reign was the formation of a Bureau of Emigration. "In 1865, Dr. Hillebrand was sent on a mission to China, India, and the Malay Archipelago, to make arrangements for the importation of labourers, to procure valuable plants and birds, and to collect information, especially in regard to leprosy. In July he sent five hundred labourers from China, under contracts with the Government, who were followed by many others. During his tour he introduced into the islands many kinds of choice plants and trees, and of insectivorous birds, and collected a large fund of useful information."*

The first hospital for lepers was established in October 1865; but I have before alluded to the dreadful disease which was first observed in the islands in 1853.

The same year, 1865, the Dowager Queen Emma sailed in Her Majesty's ship *Clio*, for

---

* I quote here, as I have often done elsewhere, from a "Brief History of the Hawaiian People," by Professor W. D. Alexander, a most interesting work, which was published by the Board of Education of the Hawaiian Kingdom.

Prince Alexander, Prince Lot, Lunalilo 189

Panama on her way to England. She spent nearly a year in England, attended by Mr. and Mrs. Hoapili Kaanuwai and Mr. C. G. Hopkins.

Kamehameha V. died in 1872, having reigned nine years. He was the last of the true Kamehamehan dynasty, and he was succeeded by Lunalilo, the highest chief by birth.

I met Queen Emma often after her return from England, she came more than once to our house to talk about England and the literature of the day, and I found her a most interesting woman. She was much beloved by the natives. So was her cousin, " Prince Bill," King Lunalilo, of only one year's reign, with whom I had a pleasant talk on European history, more than once during that period. He had a charming personality, and was popular with all classes. Genial and witty, unfortunately he was too great a favourite in society, and he drank hard at intervals. One day whilst still " Prince Bill," on coming unsteadily out of a grog shop, he met Dr. Damon, who was styled the " Father of the Pacific," a much esteemed American pastor and the seamen's chaplain. " Ha! ha!" laughed the Prince, catching the latter by the hand, " The pulpit and the bar meet!"

At a grand party on an American man-of-war which I remember well, after supper, he called on the band to "Play up Rule Britannia!" But much was forgiven to handsome Lunalilo, for he truly loved his people. At his death he left the bulk of his property to found a delightful retreat for poor and aged Hawaiians.

KING LUNALILO, "PRINCE BILL"

TO W. H.
IMMORTAL

CHAPTER IX

THE LAST OF HAWAIIAN ROYALTY

As regards the constitution of the Hawaiian kingdom, the first one was proclaimed in 1840. It confirmed the offices of Kahuna Nui—viceroy, regent, or premier, as the time demanded—and of the four governors, instituted by the first Kamehameha over the four larger islands, and it defined their powers and obligations. I have already alluded to some of these officials, such as John Young, Governor of Hawaii, Hoapili of Maui, Ruth, the rich Governess of Hawaii, &c. A legislative body was constituted, consisting of hereditary nobles and seven representatives chosen by the people. They all sat in one chamber. Four judges, appointed by this legislative body, formed a Supreme Court of Final Appeal.

A new Constitution was framed in 1852, in drafting which the king was represented by

Dr. Judd, the nobles by John Ii, a judicious and tactful native, and the representatives by Chief Justice Lee, a clever American lawyer, who had six years previously organised the Courts of Justice. The two houses now sat in different chambers—the number of representatives being not less than twenty-four, who were to be elected by universal suffrage. The office of Kuhina Nui was continued, but Kamehameha V. abolished this in 1864. He also made a property qualification necessary for the right of suffrage, and a law that all voters born since 1840 must be able to read and write. The nobles' and the peoples' representatives were again to sit in one chamber.

Lunalilo had always spoken of his cousin, Queen Emma, as his successor to the throne, but he had deferred having her proclaimed, according to law; and after a contest, during which the natives showed their desire for her as their ruler, by a short, sharp riot, which was quelled by the decision of the British and the American Ministers, who called out the marines from the British and American men-of-war in port, David Kalakaua, who took rank through his mother, was made king. He, also, was known in this country. After visiting Europe

The Last of Hawaiian Royalty

he had a gold crown made, as an insigna of royalty, in place of the traditional and dignified feather mantle of the Kamehamehas; a standing army and a native coinage were set up, but all the old Hawaiian prestige went. He attended Christian services at times; but he also consulted an old heathen sorceress, revived pagan rites, and encouraged lewd dances. He also sold, as I said before, exemptions to lepers, who ought to have been sent to Molokai. He sold an opium licence to a Chinaman, when he had already accepted an enormous bribe from another for the same licence. As he often declared, he would gladly have exchanged his throne for a good income and leave to enjoy his life in Europe. His companions and private advisers were men who had not the respect of the people, they were most of them white men utterly devoid of principle.

In June 1887 the patience of all right-minded and honourable foreigners being exhausted by the incompetence and corruption of the government under Kalakaua, at a great mass meeting they passed a resolution to the effect that "the administration of the Hawaiian Government has ceased, through corruption and incompetence, to perform those functions and afford that protection to personal and property rights for which all Governments exist," and it was exacted of the king that within twenty-four hours he should give specific pledges of future good conduct on the basis of a new Constitution.

King Kalakaua's surrender was complete. Within the appointed time, he sent a messenger to the committee appointed by the mass meeting, announcing his compliance with the demands of the citizens. He subsequently signed a new Constitution, which gave the suffrage to every male resident, whether Hawaiian or foreign, after one year's residence in the country. The nobles, or upper house, were no longer to be appointed by the Sovereign, they were to be elected by the people. The king's position became, in point of fact, almost a nominal one; and the responsibility of the Government lay with a carefully chosen Cabinet, which could only be dissolved by vote of the Legislature which was elected by the people.

And now Hawaii enjoyed six years of peaceful prosperity. Good roads were made, the harbour was improved and commerce flourished. Useless offices were done away with. Taxes were collected more systematically, and whilst securing their own rights, the foreign residents under a wise and honourable Ministry and houses of representatives, were mindful of the rights and privileges of the native Hawaiians.

In 1891 Kalakaua died. His widow Kapiolani, who was in England at the time of our Queen's Jubilee celebration, was always much respected. She was of nobler Hawaiian type than her husband, and in point of fact better born, as the last King of Kauai was her grandfather. She founded the Hawaiian Maternity Home, assisted by some of the ladies of Honolulu, and she has remained a favourite with all who knew her, both before and after her court life. Kapiolani was, later, one of the first to acknowledge that a change in the government was an absolute necessity for the well-being of her people.

Liliuokalani, Kalakaua's elder sister, succeeded to the throne. For two years she showed herself prudent, and apparently willing that all should go on in the good way which had been established. Knowing that she believed in the " divine right of kings," it was feared that she would at once have asserted herself in autocratic fashion. But after the death of her husband, Governor Dominis, an American of respectable position, Queen Liliuokalani deteriorated in many ways. During the time that I lived in Honolulu, her husband's mother, Mrs. Dominis, a person of strong and firm character, lived with the Governor and his wife, then commonly known as Princess Lydia, in a large, pleasant house near to that of her sister, the Princess Like-like, who was the wife of Mr. Cleghorn, a Scotch merchant. Their daughter—her niece and heir—the Princess Kauilani, was sent to England when she was fourteen years of age, to be educated under the guardianship of Mr. Davies, an English merchant, who was formerly our Consul in Honolulu, but who now resides in England. She was proclaimed as heir apparent in 1891, and received under the monarchical government an allowance of £500 a year.

The first false step in her government seems to have been taken when, after her husband's death, the queen appointed a Tahitian half-caste, whose name had for some time been discreditably associated with herself, to the chief executive office of Hawaii. He had been a blacksmith by trade. She gave him quarters

The Last of Hawaiian Royalty   197

in her palace, although he had his wife outside. And circumstances connected with him, and with other unworthy favourites and unscrupulous white adventurers, soon caused Liliuokalani to lose the respect and confidence of the better thinking Hawaiians, as well as of the foreigners. Such Ministers were chosen by herself as would blink at her mode of life. After three of these had been out-voted by the Legislature, the queen consented to the appointment of a Cabinet of four men of known integrity and position.

In spite of this apparent yielding—under the evil influence of her corrupt advisers—she managed by bribes and corruption to carry Bills for introducing a State lottery, and also for lessening the opium duties ; both of these measures having been protested against by deputations from respectable merchants and residents of the islands, both of native Hawaiians and of the white population.

And because they knew that the Supreme Court would declare their carrying of the lottery and opium Bills to be unconstitutional, the queen and her adventurers determined that they would have a new Constitution. This was in January 1893.

The United States cruiser *Boston*, which had been in the harbour of Honolulu, had been away at Hilo for ten days. She happened, fortunately, to return into Honolulu harbour just at a critical point, namely on the morning of the 14th, when the city had been startled by the information that Liliuokalani was announcing her intention arbitrarily to promulgate a new Constitution. The American Minister, Mr. Stevens, had also been away at Hilo with the commander of the *Boston*. On landing, he and the English Minister, Major Wodehouse, immediately tried to gain access to the queen, and to prevent her from doing what must inevitably lead to a revolution. But it was too late: things had gone too far.

Immediately after the prorogation of the Legislature at noon, the queen, attended, at her command, by the Cabinet, proceeded to the palace, to which also the leaders of the disaffected natives' party marched, in order to present the New Constitution to the queen, with the request that it should be made known to the people as the fundamental law of the land, a Constitution framed by her evil-minded advisers, in conjunction with herself.

This movement was a preconcerted one.

For the last two weeks her agents had been agitating through the islands. A great crowd of natives gathered round the palace gates, about the Government building and elsewhere. The queen, magnificently attired, and wearing a coronet of diamonds, retired with the Cabinet to the blue room of the palace, and at once presented them with a draft of this new Constitution, to which she demanded their immediate counter signatures as she declared she was resolved to promulgate it at once. All the Ministers advised her not to violate law in this fashion, and they earnestly besought her to reconsider the steps she was taking. But it was in vain. The queen brought down her clenched hand on the table at which she sat and said:

"Gentlemen, I do not wish to hear any more advice, I intend to promulgate this Constitution and to do it now." She also added that unless they conceded to her desire she should go out upon the palace steps and tell her already excited people that her Ministers were inside, refusing to allow her to grant them what they demanded. The Cabinet knew what her threat meant and they hurriedly left her and went to the Government building, whence they sent out messengers, through whom the leading citizens were hastily brought together at the office of a prominent lawyer. There they decided to resist the queen's measure to the last.

Again a long conference and struggle took place with the queen in the palace, and she was angry and excited, but at four o'clock on the same afternoon she returned to the throne room and, mounting the daïs, she spoke to the assembled officials of the Government, native members of the Legislature and others, telling them that she considered the existing Constitution faulty, but that for the present patience must be exercised, and a new Constitution would certainly be promulgated. Mr. White, her agent, replied, thanking her Majesty, assuring her of her people's love, and telling her they should wait patiently till she could fulfil her promise of giving them this new Constitution.

Then a native began a violent and inflammatory discourse. He demanded the lives of the Ministers and declared that he "thirsted for their blood."

A little later, Liliuokalani herself addressed the crowd from a balcony, telling them that "on account of the perfidy of her Ministers" she could not yet grant what they required, but it was only a case of short delay.

A "committee of public safety" was now formed, as essential to the public well-being. The revolutionist party held a meeting in the palace on the following day—Sunday—and native Hawaiian pastors were called in by the queen to pray that she might keep the throne which "evil-minded foreigners were trying to take from her." On Monday, a native mass meeting in favour of the new Constitution was held, but another immense and enthusiastic concourse of citizens, in which every class in the community was represented, passed a resolution denouncing the action of the queen and her supporters as being "unlawful, unwarranted, in derogation of the rights of the people, endangering the peace of the community, and tending to excite riot and cause loss of life and destruction of property." It was decided further that ways and means must be devised "to secure the maintenance of law and order and the protection of life, liberty, and property in Hawaii."

After this the Committee of Public Safety requested the Minister of the United States to land the men of the *Boston* lest riot and incendiarism might burst out in the night, since no reliable police force now existed, the forces being under the control of the queen and those adventurers and lottery promoters who had been the originators of the revolution.

Some have censured this action of a United States official as having been taken in order to lead to the queen's deposition; but, in point of fact, it was a step necessary for the protection of the foreign residents.

The queen now left the town, and it was at length resolved at meetings called by the Committee of Public Safety that a provisional government must be formed which should exist until some more permanent basis for the welfare of the islands could be established. Having determined to act in an unconstitutional manner, endangering the interests of the nation, Liliuokalani was, in point of fact, dethroned.

Mr. Sanford B. Dole was finally unanimously elected as the head of this provisional government. No one who knew him could question the wisdom of this selection.

There was later an attempt to restore the queen, but as it was considered to be mainly through the action of those men who were interested in the passing of the opium and the lottery Bills, it proved futile.

The day on which the New Provisional Government was proclaimed was January 17, and a day later the ex-queen wrote to President Harrison of the United States, pleading her claim to be reinstated, or, failing that, to an indemnity in money, on the score that the men of an American man-of-war had been called out to aid and abet the unlawful movements of some of her subjects, aided by aliens who had renounced their loyalty and revolted against the Constitutional government of her kingdom! These were her own words.

Nothing, however, came of this, it being proved that, as before stated, the men of the *Boston* had only been landed for the protection of American subjects during a time of riot.

Out of the Provisional Government grew the Republic, with Mr. Sanford Dole, who had the confidence of all parties, as its President.

In January of 1895, however, a more serious revolution threatened, and there was an attempt to put the queen back on the throne. Ammunition and rifles were brought from San Francisco in a sealing schooner, and a half-caste became the military leader. His first "aide" was another half-caste, who had a military education in Italy, and who had, in 1889, led a disgraceful, but futile, revolutionary movement against her brother, Kalakaua. Little has been said about this by Hawaiian writers, but it resulted in some loss of life.

A large quantity of arms were stored at the ex-queen's home, the old Dominis' house, called Washington Place. Giant powder bombs were made, and were found later in an underground receptacle at the back of Liliuokalani's house, with ammunition. Some of the bomb-shells were made of cement, four were of iron, and there was one large bomb with a coco-nut shell. A fragment of a shell was found on the ex-queen's writing-desk.

The Government received information from a spy that arms had been landed, and that a quantity was stored in a house near Diamond Head, and half a dozen native police went with Captain Parker to make a search there. Whilst Deputy Brown was reading the search-warrant to Bertelmann, a half-caste contractor who owned the house, shooting began outside, the rebel natives commencing the attack.

Poor Charles Carter, a fine young man, who, with his cousin, had followed the party of police to Bertelmann's, was shot dead. He was a grandson of Dr. Judd, and his death was felt deeply by the whole community.

And so a short, sharp war began; it only lasted ten days, but it was a time of terrible anxiety. The end of it was the abject submission of the leaders, all of them being either half-castes or a low class of white adventurers.

The last view we have of their General is in his cell, weeping like a child, and offering to make a complete disclosure of the whole plot, which the authorities did not, however, care to hear. A half-caste ranchman was the most picturesque figure of the leaders of the party. He is considered to be the handsomest man on the islands, is over six feet in height, well made, with fine features, and immensely strong. His father claimed descent from the old kings of Ireland, and his mother is said to have the blood of the old Kamehamehas in her veins. A stonemason was another leading man, but the manager of a harness shop was the only pure foreigner in the party.

Before the queen was arrested she had contrived to destroy a large quantity of papers, but there was evidence at the subsequent trials that plans had been made for the blowing up of the largest foreign church, of the executive and other buildings, and also the wholesale massacre of all who had had the slightest connection with the existing Government.

For a time Liliuokalani was under arrest in the palace, but she was afterwards allowed to retire as Mrs. Dominis, a private citizen, to her own house, Washington Place.

She executed first a document containing an abdication and renunciation of all sovereign rights heretofore claimed, which she states was made "after full and free consultation with my personal friends and with my legal advisers . . . and also upon my own free volition and in pursuance of my unalterable belief and understanding of my duty to the people of Hawaii, and to their highest and best interests, and also for the sake of those misguided Hawaiians and others who have recently engaged in rebellion against the Republic, and in an attempt to restore me to the position of queen."

In the same document she says: "I hereby do fully and unequivocally admit and declare that the Government of the Republic of Hawaii is the lawful Government of the Hawaiian Islands, and that the late Hawaiian Monarchy is finally and for ever ended," &c. &c.

Further, the ex-queen stated that she for ever abdicated not only for herself, but for her heirs and successors; and that it was her "sincere desire henceforth to live in absolute privacy, and retirement from all publicity, or even appearance of being concerned in the public affairs of the Hawaiian Islands, further than to express, as I do now, and shall always continue to do, my most sincere hope for the welfare and prosperity of Hawaii and its people under and subject to the Government of the Republic of Hawaii," &c. &c.

That the ex-queen has not respected this document, which she states was executed by her own free volition, is now well known.

CHAPTER X

THE HAWAII OF TO-DAY

JAPAN has often been called the "Children's Paradise" but Hawaii has quite as good a title to the name, for all children look upon outdoor life as the best of all life, and the young people of Hawaii are constantly in the open; morning, noon and evening they bathe in air and sunshine. Even when it rains, the little ones can play on the broad verandah while the older ones read or write or sew there.

At thirteen or fourteen many boys are allowed to go out camping under the care of elder brothers or cousins. A party of eight or more will arrange to go for a week or ten days in the Easter or midsummer holidays, each one promising to bring some contribution to the housekeeping. Perhaps one boy is fortunate enough

The Hawaii of To-day

to have a father who possesses a tent, or, if not, some other boy is able to borrow one. Some undertake to bring fryingpan, saucepan, kettle and tin plates, knives, forks and spoons, others bring flour, bread, butter, lard, eggs, tins of jelly and meats, and each one must be provided with a blanket and a change of clothing. These are packed in saddle-bags or sacks, and loaded on a pack mule, or strong pony, and the boys, in their oldest clothes, either on foot or horseback, set out before dawn, in order to get early to their happy hunting-grounds in the woods, or on the mountains where they enjoy their holidays to the fullest extent, shooting wild turkeys and ducks, chickens, and occasionally pheasants and goats, hunting for rare ferns and tree-shells, for in these wondrous islands shells grow on trees. These are really snail shells, but, unlike our dull English ones, they are most brilliant in colour, in all the varying shades of the rainbow. Of the land shells there are one thousand different varieties, many of them perfectly unique. An Italian Professor of the University of Pisa, Cavaliere Regnoli, with whom we once travelled up the Mexican coast, told me that he intended, some time, to make a special journey

o

from Italy, in order to get for himself a collection of the land shells of Hawaii.

There are many rare ferns also to be found on the mountains and in the woods, maidenhair growing luxuriantly beneath the banks of the streams, where the floods have hollowed out the water-course above their usual height. Including rare and common ones, the islands can boast one hundred and fifty varieties.

All the young people learn very early to ride, and parties of boys and girls take advantage of the wonderfully bright moonlight evenings to make up riding parties together. The horses are very sure-footed and gallop down, as well as up hill, in a style that new comers often think very risky.

Three miles from the city is a pleasant seaside resort, Waikiki, which was once frequented by the Kamehamehas, many of whose royal fishponds were there. Now, most of the Honolulu business men own, or rent, a house for a few weeks each year, either here or at some other place on the coast, but this is the most popular as well as the most accessible from the metropolis.

The sea being on every hand the boys and girls of Hawaii learn early to swim and row,

and the island-born foreigners emulate the natives in their surf-board riding, canoeing and fishing by torchlight. The latter pastime affords a curious spectacle, the dark shore lit up here and there by the flaming torches held on high to attract the fish to the net, and the excited group of barefooted lads and lasses gathered around the flashing light. Then, when they return home, there is the pouring out of the brightly coloured contents of the net at the foot of the verandah steps, amidst excited exclamations of "three squid," "four ama-ama" (the native name for grey mullet) and many more names unknown and untranslatable to English ears. The native fish are brilliant in colouring, past everything that those who have not seen them could imagine.

The young girls of Honolulu, like their European and American sisters, form themselves into societies for amusement and charitable purposes. One of these some time ago got up what they called a fan drill band; making pretty frocks of gaily coloured chintzes and cottons. Sticking small fans in their powdered hair and taking larger ones in their hands, they perfected themselves in a sort of drill and then gave performances for some local charity.

There has been for a long time a Honolulu Hospital Flower Society which every week takes flowers to the hospital which Queen Emma founded for the benefit of her people, where all natives are cared for without any charge, and foreigners for a very small fee. The committee for the distribution of flowers is usually composed of young girls, though occasionally older women are associated with them in the pleasant work.

The foreign children quickly catch up the little Hawaiian songs and a small guitar-like instrument which the natives call an "Uke lele" (literary "jumping flea") makes a pretty light accompaniment to their childish voices as they sit at the foot of a great "inga" or some leafy mango tree, amusing themselves and others by the hour.

The mothers of these fortunate white children are anxious to make life as pleasant as possible for the native children also; and to this end, they interest themselves much in their education. In the next house to my sister's Waikiki home, lived a native family whose father was paralysed, and, fearing that a little bright-eyed girl of seven, who was continually peering through the fence, did not get enough to eat, my sister offered to put her into one of the mission schools. At first the mother was unwilling to part with the child and declined to let her go, saying she had never been used to sleeping on anything but a mat, and she was sure she would fall out of the beds they had in the school, but at last she consented, and the little creature was placed under the care of the good teachers at Kawaiahao, where she is now a promising pupil of twelve.

The same sister, finding that the natives around her mountain home, some three years ago, had no school near enough for the very little ones to go to, started a free Kindergarten for one hour each morning, and in this she was helped by two young white girls of about eighteen, who each took one day a week. At Christmas she gave these children and those of the Sunday school in her neighbourhood, a Christmas tree with refreshments of ice cream and cake, to which they all eagerly looked forward from one year's end to another. This Kindergarten is now no longer needed, as a good Government school has been built close to the building where the Kindergarten was held.

The Government school system is equal to that of any in the world, and it is supplemented at Punahou, at the entrance of the beautiful Manoa Valley, two miles from the city, by a school which was first begun for the children of the missionaries, but very quickly gathered in others. In the early days the distance from town was a great drawback to the day pupils, as all the parents were not able to provide horses and saddles for their children. This difficulty, however, was remedied by a two-horse bus, which, starting from a valley on the opposite side of Honolulu, gathered in the boys and girls by a tootling horn. The bus is now superseded by the universal tramcar.

The stone wall behind Punahou school buildings is covered with the night-blooming cereus—a cactus which grows so luxuriantly that as many as from eight to ten thousand have been seen to open in one night. The blossoms often measure twelve inches in diameter. Standing by this hedge one can watch flower after flower gently open, till very soon the whole fence is one mass of fairy-like beauty, which can only be realised by one who has actually beheld it.

Behind my sister's grounds in Nuuanu Valley

are also trailing plants of these large cereus starry blossoms. A feature of many of the gardens, is a pleasant stream running through their midst, bordered by luxuriant tradescantia, and often alive with gold fish which are native to the islands. When, after rain in the mountains, a freshet comes down some of the streams, the scene is a very lively one.

A large building, almost in the centre of the town, which was a palace of Princess Ruth's (once Governess of Hawaii and the richest native of her time) left by her to the Princess Bernice Pauahi (Mrs. Charles Bishop) has been bought by the Board of Education and converted into a high school. Here very many foreign and native children are studying. Incorporated with it is a normal school, where young men and women, Hawaiian, English and American, are training as teachers for the coming years. The education in the free schools of Hawaii would surprise an Englishman.

There are native lawyers and judges, and the great majority of compositors and pressmen in the printing offices are Hawaiians. Some are also sugar planters, schoolmasters, clergymen, and government officials, and engineers; in fact everything is open to them.

Some of our papers have called the members of the late Provisional Government of Hawaii "a band of filibusters," yet the census returns just published show that the number of pure Hawaiians owning real estate, has increased in the last six years from 3271 to 3995, that is, 22 per cent., although during the same time the Hawaiians had decreased at the rate of ten per cent.

According to the latest census, that taken in 1896, the population of the island was 109,020; of these, 72,517 were males, and 36,503 females; the number of pure native Hawaiians was 30,975. The number of pure Hawaiian men is much in excess of the women, and this has always been a great source of trouble. The latter, those in and near the towns especially, often prefer the Chinamen and Japanese as husbands, because these are more industrious, providing for them better than do the indolent natives. A very hopeful and intelligent race of half-castes has been the result of these intermarriages, but they have been a bitter root of heartburnings and jealous quarrels. It was found also necessary, soon after foreign vessels began to visit the islands, to make a law that no foreigner who was married to a native should leave the kingdom without a formal, written, and duly witnessed permission from his wife.

This reminds me of the native lady, the notary, Mrs. Emma Nakuina, who has been investigating lately the story of the present oldest inhabitant, a still vigorous, old woman of at least 122—she says herself, 124—years of age. She is now deaf but not blind, and her chief attendant is the wife of a grandson. Her memory is very clear and she can tell of most of the important events of her time. Apau, as she is called, was an attendant on Kapiolani when she descended into the crater to break the tabu, and a child when Captain Cook arrived in the islands. The surname of Apau was given her after the defiance of the goddess Pele. It means "You will be eaten up," which was prophesied of Kapiolani and her attendants as a punishment for their temerity. An amusing incident told by her family is, that Kapiolani, being jealous of her great beauty, ordered her hair to be cut and combed evenly over her face, so as to conceal part of this. And she would not allow her to be married for many years.

Converted to Christianity with her mistress, she was taught to read English at the same time, and she has been a great reader of the Bible until her sight failed, at the age of at least 120. She took in washing until very recently, but gave it up because the Chinamen were absorbing the business. Her appetite was pretty good at 122, and she says that, had she not slipped in a bath-room and dislocated a bone, she would still be useful.

The chief exports of Hawaii are sugar, rice, coffee, bananas, wool, hides, pine-apples, molasses, bone and horns. Of these over 95 per cent. go to the United States.

Mr. A. F. Judd, a judge in Honolulu, held in high esteem by the English as well as the Americans, wrote truly in 1881 : "It would be difficult to find a country where the sentiment of nationality is stronger than among the aboriginal Hawaiians ; but the preservation of the native Government is due, not so much to this sentiment as to the unwavering efforts of the early foreign advisers of Kamehameha III. to maintain the Hawaiian State, independent of dictation, free from protectorates, and without 'residents' of foreign Powers. Between 1830 and 1850 there were several crises, when a single miss-step, or even a single deflection from loyalty to principle on the part of the king's advisers would have been fatal to the existence of the kingdom."

But the third Kamehameha was a man who never compromised his country nor disclosed State secrets, even in one of those unfortunate periodical revels during which drink made him mad; nor did he ever entrust important offices to men of loose morals or corrupt principles—as was done in recent Hawaiian history. Although he never professed himself to be a religious man, he always treated Christianity with respect, and attended its services; telling his people to follow its precepts and not to copy his example. Indeed, as I have already told, one of his first public acts was "the solemn dedication of his kingdom to the Lord Jesus Christ."

A Hawaiian author, commenting on this, says: "A book of remembrance is kept, and let the future of the Hawaiian nation be what it may, the King of Kings will regard the record."

www.ingramcontent.com/pod-product-compliance
Lightning Source LLC
Chambersburg PA
CBHW031743230426
43669CB00007B/465